Poetry of Redemption

Poetry of Redemption

AN **ILLUSTRATED TREASURY**
OF **GOOD FRIDAY** AND
EASTER POEMS

Leland Ryken

P&R
PUBLISHING
P.O. BOX 817 • PHILLIPSBURG • NEW JERSEY 08865-0817

Scripture quotations marked (KJV) are taken from the King James Version.

A Scripture quotation from the New Testament uses the ESV's alternate, footnoted translation of *adelphoi* ("brothers and sisters").

Italics within Scripture quotations indicate emphasis added.

Printed in the United States of America

Library of Congress Cataloging-in-Publication Data

Names: Ryken, Leland, editor.
Title: Poetry of redemption : An illustrated treasury of Good Friday and Easter poems / [edited by] Leland Ryken.
Description: Phillipsburg, New Jersey : P&R Publishing, [2023] | Summary: "This beautiful anthology features readings on the events of Holy Week and our response. Ryken examines forty hymns, poems, and Scripture texts in a celebration of their artistry and meaning"-- Provided by publisher.

Identifiers: LCCN 2022045278 | ISBN 9781629959757 (paperback) | ISBN 9781629959511 (epub)
Subjects: LCSH: Holy Week--Prayers and devotions. | Holy Week--Meditations. | Jesus Christ--Passion--Meditations. | Christian poetry.
Classification: LCC BV90 .T74 2023 | DDC 263/.925--dc23/eng/20221207
LC record available at https://lccn.loc.gov/2022045278

FOR PHILIP AND LISA

Eric Gill, *The Resurrection*, 1917

Contents

Gerbrand van den Eeckhout,
The Last Supper, 1664

Pieter Brueghel the Younger,
The Crucifixion, ca. 1617

Introduction

THIS BOOK IS AN ANTHOLOGY of poetic devotionals on the events of Holy Week and their meaning. Although the entries can be read in the days before and during Holy Week, the book is not organized according to a schedule of daily readings tied to the calendar. One can read this anthology anytime, using any timetable, covering as many of the entries at a single reading as one chooses.

Three types of texts make up the readings. They correspond to the three categories listed in a famous New Testament passage that enjoins Christians to address one another "in psalms and hymns and spiritual songs" (Eph. 5:19). This anthology uses the designation *psalms* to refer to poems that are (a) taken from the Bible and (b) printed in the verse form of all biblical poetry, namely, parallelism of phrases and clauses. It uses the designation *hymns* to refer to the texts of familiar Holy Week songs, which are here presented and analyzed as devotional poems. We need to remind ourselves that every hymn begins its life as a poem, becoming a hymn only when it is paired with music and sung. The "spiritual songs" in this anthology are classic literary poems, written by the "greats" of English poetry, on the sacrifice and resurrection of Jesus.

The table of contents shows how the organization of this anthology follows the chronology of Holy Week. The contents are balanced between describing what happened during Holy Week and applying those events in the lives of believers.

The overall genre of this anthology is variously called devotional literature and meditative or contemplative literature. Devotional literature is designed to fix our thoughts on God and the spiritual life and to awaken our religious affections. This is the intended orientation and goal of the entries in this anthology.

Master of the Death of Saint Nicholas of Münster, *Calvary*, ca. 1470/80

To call the entries meditative or contemplative identifies the means by which their devotional effect is achieved. The basic structure of a meditative work was codified by a method that dates back to the Middle Ages. Its three-phase procedure is all but inevitable. The first phase is called *composing the scene,* which refers to recalling an event from the Bible and imagining oneself being present at it. The second phase consists of analyzing the details that make up the scene and event. Whereas composing the scene is based on memory and imagination, the second phase—*analysis of meaning*—is rooted in understanding. The third phase is *response.* We today might call it an *action plan.* It activates our will to respond with thanksgiving, resolve, and the expression of other feelings and by petitioning God.

It is impossible to overstate the importance of this meditative paradigm to the entries in this anthology. Because the foundation of the poems is the events of Holy Week, most of the poems contain some element of composing the scene. But the strategy of the poets is never merely to recreate the events. Instead, their poems lead us to analyze the spiritual meanings of those events and then prompt us to respond appropriately.

Although the contemplative paradigm places the three phases in a sequential order, the mixture is much more fluid in poems and hymns. Often the phases are repeated in individual stanzas of a poem and do not determine the structure of the poem as a whole. What matters for us as readers is that we keep the three ingredients—composing the scene, analyzing the meaning, responding—in our awareness.

This helps us to understand the devotional nature of the content in this theology, but how are we to understand its *poetic* nature? Five aspects of poetry must be kept firmly in mind.

Poetry arranges its content into lines. In prose, the sentence is the recurrent unit, and the flow of text runs all the way to the right margin of the page and then wraps around to the left margin. Thoughts in poetry are packaged into lines, a much more compressed form of expression that gives more "bang for the buck" than prose sentences do. This requires more careful attention on the part of the reader. The packaging of content into lines and groups of lines is also more artful than prose, displaying skill in the handling of language and syntax (sentence structure).

Poetry is packaged in the form of stanzas. The arrangement of poetic lines into stanzas gives them another layer of tightness and control. Individual stanzas possess a unity within themselves. They are not random

collections of details. We therefore need to analyze how a stanza is organized, including what constitutes the unity of a stanza.

Poems are organized on a principle of theme and variation. Every well-composed poem has a unifying theme or "big idea." In the overwhelming number of instances, we can trust the poem's first line or two to clue us into its unifying theme. Everything that follows expands on that theme. Rather than repeating their main ideas, poets *elaborate* on them through variations within stanzas. Thus we need to analyze how individual stanzas contribute to the elaboration of a poem's main idea.

Poems express ideas in images and figures of speech. Whereas prose, such as the prose of this introduction, tends toward an abstract vocabulary, poetry names concrete things and actions (*images*). In addition, poets tend to think in terms of *analogy*, in which one thing is compared

Benjamin West, *Angel of the Resurrection*, 1801

to another. Metaphor, simile, and symbol are common forms of such comparison. Because poets think in images and figures of speech, so must we as readers. We need to take the time, and expend the mental energy, required to unpack the meanings that are embodied in individual images and comparisons. Poetry requires a slow read.

Poetry is expressed in rhythm and rhyme. All the poems in this anthology are written in regular rhythm or *meter,* and most of them employ rhyming sounds at the ends of their lines. These constitute the music of poetry and are part of its verbal beauty. The effects of sound are part of the experience of poetry, even in silent reading, but the effects are largely unnoticed. We do not need to analyze the meter and rhyme scheme of a poem to experience it fully, though it is pleasurable to do so. Regardless of our level of analysis, we need to credit poets for casting utterances into smooth-flowing, regular meter and ending their poetic lines with rhyming sounds that follow a set pattern from one stanza to the next.

Each of the poems in this anthology is accompanied by an *explication.* This is the term used by literary scholars to describe a literary analysis and explanation of the form and content of a poem. A good explication is not a random collection of insights but an organized exploration. We can think of an explicator as a tour guide who chooses what sites to visit, who points and says, "Look at that," and who interprets what the tourists are seeing.

The explications in this anthology are comprised of (1) a brief context for the poem, including where appropriate its author and composition; (2) a statement of the unifying theme of the poem and an analysis of how the individual stanzas are variations on that theme; (3) a discussion of the poem's artistic effects and verbal beauty; (4) an exploration of the theological content of the poem, with an eye on how the poem relates to the main focus of this anthology, namely, the sacrifice and resurrection of Jesus; and (5) a concluding sentence or two that makes the poem's devotional takeaway explicit.

The best way to combine each devotional passage with its explication is first to read the devotional entry, then to read the explication as a way of reaching a fuller understanding and enjoyment of the work, and then to read the devotional a second time, using the explication as a lens through which to view the passage. Each entry also includes a passage from the Bible that brings the entire poem and explication under a unifying umbrella, stated with the authority that only the Bible can offer. ■

PROLOGUE

The prayers that comprise this prologue are a portal through which we may enter both Holy Week and this anthology. They show us at a glance that the events of Holy Week move from Palm Sunday to Good Friday to Easter and direct our attention to the anticipated resurrection at the last day. ■

Fernando Gallego, *The Agony in the Garden*
(detail), 1480–88

Prayers for Holy Week

Book of Common Prayer

Palm Sunday

Blessed is the King
 who comes in the name of the Lord.
Assist us mercifully with your help,
 O Lord God of our salvation,
that we may enter with joy
 upon the contemplation of your mighty acts,
whereby you have given us life and immortality,
 through Jesus Christ our Lord.
It is right to praise you, Almighty God,
 for the acts of love by which you have redeemed us
 through your Son Jesus Christ our Lord.

On this day he entered the holy city of Jerusalem in triumph,
 and was proclaimed as King of kings
by those who spread their garments
 and branches of palm along his way.
Let these branches be for us signs of his victory,
 and grant that we who bear them in his name
may ever hail him as our King,
 and follow him in the way that leads to eternal life.

Good Friday

Almighty God, we pray you graciously
to behold us your family,
for whom our Lord Jesus Christ was willing to be betrayed,
and given into the hands of sinners,
and to suffer death upon the cross,
who now lives and reigns with you and the Holy Spirit,
one God, forever and ever.

Our heavenly Father sent his Son into the world,
not to condemn the world,
but that the world through him might be saved,
that all who believe in him
might be delivered from the power of sin and death,
and become heirs with him of everlasting life.

Lord Jesus Christ, Son of the living God,
we pray you to set your passion, cross, and death
between your judgment and our souls,
now and in the hour of our death.
Give mercy and grace to the living;
pardon and rest to the dead;
to your holy church peace and concord;
and to us sinners everlasting life and glory.

Holy Saturday

O God, Creator of heaven and earth,
grant that, as the crucified body of your dear Son
was laid in the tomb and rested on this holy Sabbath,
so we may await with him the coming of the third day,
and rise with him to newness of life.

Easter

Almighty God, who through thine only-begotten Son
hast overcome death
and opened unto us the gate of everlasting life,
grant, we beseech thee, that we may be found worthy
to attain to everlasting joys,
through Jesus Christ our Lord,
who liveth and reigneth with thee
and the Holy Ghost forever,
one God, world without end.

Grant, O Lord, that through the gate of death
we may pass to our joyful resurrection,
through his merits, who died, and was buried,
and rose again for us,
thy Son, Jesus Christ our Lord.

We humbly beseech thee, O Father,
to raise us from the death of sin
unto the life of righteousness;
that, when we shall depart this life,
we may rest in him;
and that, at the general resurrection in the last day,
we may be found acceptable in thy sight,
and receive that blessing,
which thy well-beloved Son shall then pronounce
to all who love and fear thee. ■

The purpose of a devotional is to orient us toward God and ultimately to unite us to him. What better way to achieve that goal than to address God directly through prayer? The fact that the prayers in today's reading are phrased in the plural offers an additional blessing. We are aware as we read that we are joining the church universal in expressing our thoughts, but this in no way reduces the personal application since we are also expressing what we feel and believe as individuals.

As we will see in every entry of this anthology, poets are our representatives. They say what we ourselves wish to say, only they say it better. Today's entry demonstrates this truth to a preeminent degree.

Reading a prayer as a devotion take us beyond simply praying it. To ponder the truth of what we are reading is inherent to devotional contemplation, so when we read the poetic fragments printed above, we can take as long as we need to understand their ideas, subject them to analysis and reflection, and codify our responses. As we reflect on individual statements from the prayer book, we need to see how what is expressed in prayer correlates with the events of Holy Week. We should ask, "Why *this* particular assertion or petition in light of Palm Sunday or Good Friday or Easter?"

Is the Book of Common Prayer poetic? It is. Much of its beauty is due to what is technically called *cadence*—the rise and fall of language and phrases. Even when it is printed as prose, we feel intuitively that its short phrases and clauses are just asking to be printed as poetic lines and stanzas. The prayer book was written in the same era as the King James Bible, and both are the very essence of verbal beauty—elegant in style, sweeping us up into something beautiful and grand. We leave our reading feeling that we have been in the presence of something great.

This devotional entry has a twofold takeaway: it ensures that the entire sweep of Holy Week is fixed in our minds as a coherent whole, and it leads us to ponder the individual events of that week and their spiritual meaning for our lives. ■

The following passage covers the broad sweep of Holy Week in a manner similar to the entry from the Book of Common Prayer: "For I delivered to you as of first importance what I also received: that Christ died for our sins in accordance with the Scriptures, that he was buried, that he was raised on the third day in accordance with the Scriptures" (1 Cor. 15:3–4).

Georges de La Tour, *The Repentant Magdalen*, ca. 1635/40

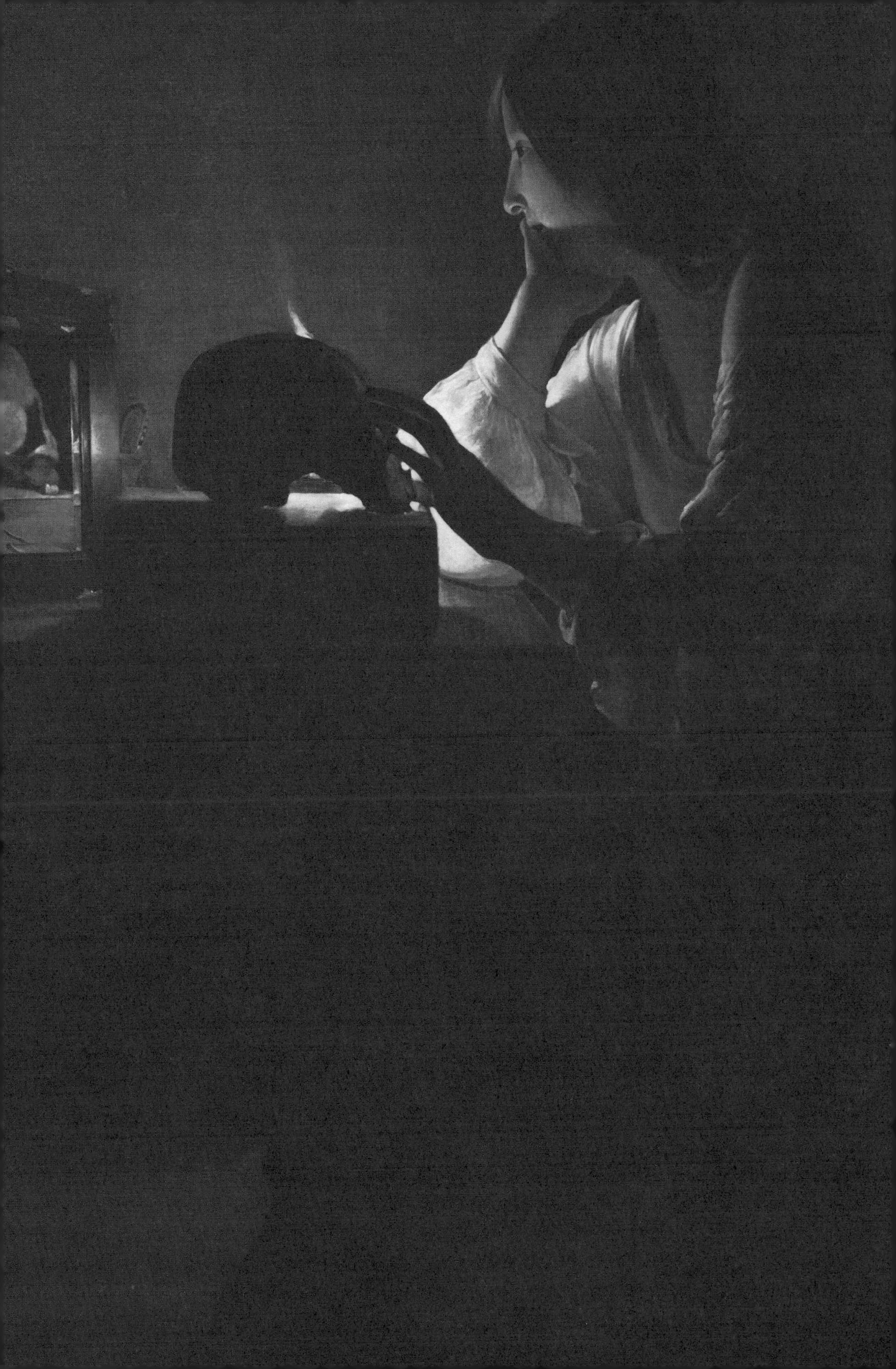

BEFORE THE FOUNDATION OF THE WORLD

GOD'S ETERNAL REDEMPTIVE PLAN

We see from Scripture that God's plan from all eternity has been to redeem fallen humanity. The four selections in this section highlight this storyline.

The passage from *Paradise Lost* imagines a dialogue between the Father and Son in which the Son volunteers to rescue the fallen human race.

Psalm 22 expresses the experience of suffering humanity; because it describes the future passion of Jesus so exactly, it assumes the quality of a prophecy.

It is followed by the psalm of the Suffering Servant from Isaiah 53, a prophecy of the nature of the coming Messiah's atoning death.

Even though it looks back at Christ's redemptive life rather than forward to it, the Christ hymn from Philippians gives us a "behind the scenes" view of Good Friday and Easter in the same way the Old Testament prophecies do. ■

Maximilian Wolf, *The Milky Way*, ca. 1900

Shall Grace Not Find Means?

John Milton (1608–1674)

Beyond compare the Son of God was seen
Most glorious; in him all his Father shone
Substantially expressed; and in his face
Divine compassion visibly appeared,
Love without end, and without measure grace,
Which uttering, thus he to his Father spoke.

". . . Should man finally be lost, should man,
Thy creature late so loved, thy youngest son,
Fall circumvented thus by fraud, though joined
With his own folly? That be from thee far,
That far be from thee, Father, who art judge
Of all things made, and judgest only right.
Or shall the Adversary thus obtain
His end, and frustrate thine? Shall he fulfill
His malice, and thy goodness bring to naught,
. . . . and to hell
Draw after him the whole race of mankind,
By him corrupted? or wilt thou thyself
Abolish thy creation, and unmake
For him, what for thy glory thou hast made?"

To whom the great Creator thus replied:
"O Son, in whom my soul hath chief delight,
Son of my bosom, Son who art alone
My word, my wisdom, and effectual might,
All hast thou spoken as my thoughts are, all
As my eternal purpose hath decreed;
Man shall not quite be lost, but saved who will;
Yet not of will in him, but grace in me,
Freely vouchsafed; once more I will renew
His lapsed powers, though forfeit; and enthralled
By sin to foul exorbitant desires;
Upheld by me, yet once more he shall stand
On even ground against his mortal foe,
By me upheld. . . . .
. . . . Man disobeying,
. . . With his whole posterity must die,
Die he or justice must; unless for him
Some other able, and as willing, pay
The rigid satisfaction, death for death.
Say, heavenly powers, where shall we find such love?
Which of you will be mortal, to redeem
Man's mortal crime, and just the unjust to save?
Dwells in all heaven charity so dear?"

Silence was in heaven, on man's behalf.
He asked, but all the heavenly choir stood mute,
Patron or intercessor none appeared. . . .
And now without redemption all mankind
Must have been lost, adjudged to death and hell
By doom severe, had not the Son of God,
In whom the fulness dwells of love divine,
His dearest mediation thus renewed.

"Father, thy word is past, man shall find grace;
And shall grace not find means? . . . .
Behold me then: me for him, life for life
I offer: on me let thine anger fall;
Account me man; I for his sake will leave
Thy bosom, and this glory next to thee
Freely put off, and for him lastly die
Well pleased; on me let death wreak all his rage.
Under his gloomy power I shall not long
Lie vanquished. . . . .
Though now to death I yield, and am his due,
Thou wilt not leave me in the loathsome grave
His prey, nor suffer my unspotted soul
Forever with corruption there to dwell;
But I shall rise victorious, and subdue
My vanquisher, spoiled of his vaunted spoil.
Death his death's wound shall then receive." ■

THIS PASSAGE FROM JOHN MILTON'S *Paradise Lost* enacts a convention esteemed in epics and known as the *council of the gods*. In the works of Homer and Virgil, the divine beings hold regular meetings on Mount Olympus to take stock of what is happening in human affairs and to decide whether they will intervene or leave people to their own designs. Milton Christianizes this convention by making it what theologians call an *intra-trinitarian dialogue* between the Father and the Son. The human crisis that occasions this "dialogue in heaven" (as Milton scholars call it) is the fall of the human race due to Satan's deception, and it leads the Son to express his willingness to become incarnate and die a substitutionary death for humankind.

Benjamin West, *The Expulsion of Adam and Eve from Paradise*, 1791

The dialogue captures perfectly what the medieval theologian Athanasius called "the divine dilemma" in his famous treatise *On the Incarnation*. Athanasius wrote, "As, then, the [human race was] wasting away and [God's] noble works perishing, what was God who is good to do? . . . It was impossible . . . to leave man to be carried off by corruption, because it would be unfitting and unworthy of God's goodness." Milton agreed, and he composed an episode in his epic to embody that dilemma.

The dialogue that Milton imagined is structured as a problem and its solution. The Father represents the voice of judgment: humankind broke God's law and therefore deserves the death that he imposed as a penalty. This is summarized in the Father's statement *Die he or justice must.* As we meditate on the events of our redemption, this needs to be the first thing that we absorb—the dilemma that necessitated the Son's sacrifice. When we realize that we are the dilemma that God needs to resolve, it should evoke in us a spirit of contrition.

In Milton's imagined dialogue, the Son represents the voice of mercy and grace. The point of greatest suspense in Milton's narrative is the moment in which no heavenly being is willing to undertake the rescue of the human race. As we contemplate this moment, we ask the question expressed by Scottish theologian Thomas Chalmers: "What could I do, if God did not justify the ungodly?" Then comes the even more moving moment when the Son asks, *And shall grace not find means?* The mystery of the substitutionary atonement is captured in the first-person pronouns of the Son's offer: *Behold me then: me for him, life for life I offer: on me let thine anger fall; account me man.*

Whereas we often celebrate all that Christ's atonement achieved for us, Milton's composition leads us to ponder the question of what would have happened if Christ had not intervened to save us. ■

The dialogue that Milton envisions highlights the extreme generosity that led the Son to sacrifice himself for unworthy people. Romans 5:6–8 sounds the same keynote:

> For while we were still weak, at the right time Christ died for the ungodly. For one will scarcely die for a righteous person—though perhaps for a good person one would dare even to die—but God shows his love for us in that while we were still sinners, Christ died for us.

The Sufferer's Psalm

Psalm 22

My God, my God, why have you forsaken me?
  Why are you so far from saving me, from the words of my groaning?
O my God, I cry by day, but you do not answer,
  and by night, but I find no rest.

Yet you are holy,
  enthroned on the praises of Israel.
In you our fathers trusted;
  they trusted, and you delivered them.
To you they cried and were rescued;
  in you they trusted and were not put to shame.
But I am a worm and not a man,
  scorned by mankind and despised by the people.
All who see me mock me;
  they make mouths at me; they wag their heads;
"He trusts in the Lord; let him deliver him;
  let him rescue him, for he delights in him!"
Yet you are he who took me from the womb;
  you made me trust you at my mother's breasts.
On you was I cast from my birth,
  and from my mother's womb you have been my God.
Be not far from me,
  for trouble is near,
  and there is none to help.
Many bulls encompass me;
  strong bulls of Bashan surround me;
they open wide their mouths at me,
  like a ravening and roaring lion.
I am poured out like water,
  and all my bones are out of joint;
my heart is like wax;
  it is melted within my breast;

my strength is dried up like a potsherd,
  and my tongue sticks to my jaws;
  you lay me in the dust of death.
For dogs encompass me;
  a company of evildoers encircles me;
they have pierced my hands and feet—
  I can count all my bones—
they stare and gloat over me;
they divide my garments among them,
  and for my clothing they cast lots.

But you, O Lord, do not be far off!
  O you my help, come quickly to my aid!
Deliver my soul from the sword,
  my precious life from the power of the dog!
  Save me from the mouth of the lion!
You have rescued me from the horns of the wild oxen!

I will tell of your name to my brothers;
  in the midst of the congregation I will praise you:
You who fear the Lord, praise him!
  All you offspring of Jacob, glorify him,
  and stand in awe of him, all you offspring of Israel!

For he has not despised or abhorred
  the affliction of the afflicted,
and he has not hidden his face from him,
  but has heard, when he cried to him.
From you comes my praise in the great congregation;
  my vows I will perform before those who fear him.
The afflicted shall eat and be satisfied;
  those who seek him shall praise the Lord!
  May your hearts live forever! ■

PSALM 22 MAKES A UNIQUE contribution to our meditation on Jesus' suffering on the cross, yet in order to understand this properly we must first study the passage in its original context. The psalm is an autobiographical poem composed by David. A headnote further humanizes the poem by expressing the poet's request that the choirmaster match the text to music that is titled (to our very great surprise) "The Doe of the Dawn."

The category into which fall the greatest number of songs in the book of Psalms is the *lament*, which the writers themselves more often called a *complaint*. Laments have a fixed form that contains five ingredients, and Psalm 22 is a "textbook model" of this form. The ingredients are (1) an introductory cry to God, which is seen in stanza 1 as printed above; (2) the complaint itself, which defines the crisis in stanza 2; (3) a petition to God to act, as in stanza 3; (4) a vow to praise God, as seen in stanza 4; and (5) a statement of confidence in God, seen in stanza 5.

Psalm 22 carries the authentic voice of suffering, but it is not expressed as only one person's experience. The poetic form of the utterance

Copy after Paulus Potter,
Bellowing Bull, 17th century

universalizes it so that it becomes an expression of suffering humanity in all times and places. The poem's metaphors similarly universalize its assertions. When the poet compares enemies to *bulls* and *lions* and physical pain to *bones* that are *out of joint*, anyone can walk into the poem and make it his or her own.

This is where the Good Friday overlay enters the picture. Because the metaphors in the poem are open-ended in application, Psalm 22 becomes an extended meditation on the physical, mental, and spiritual agony that Jesus suffered on the cross. Many of the details in the psalm match his agony at Calvary, and Jesus himself quoted from it while on the cross.

Two important applications of the poem emerge. First, the suffering that Jesus endured was greater than that of other people, but it was nonetheless human suffering such as we know. According to Isaiah 53:4, Jesus bore not only our sins but also our griefs. As Hebrews 4:15 states, "We do not have a high priest who is unable to sympathize with our weaknesses."

The second application stems from the fact that lament psalms do not only define a crisis and give vent to the agony of suffering but also counterbalance the suffering with statements of confidence in God and vows to praise him for the victory that he ultimately gives. Psalm 22 ends in triumph. We should not think that Good Friday was a defeat and Easter a victory. The psalm reminds us that the cross was the means of Christ's victory over Satan and over the penalty of sin.

If we follow the contour outlined above, Psalm 22 can move us to a deeper understanding of the suffering Jesus experienced during his passion. ■

We understand Psalm 22 to be a poem of the cross to the degree to which we can identify its parallels to the events of Jesus' crucifixion. One of the psalm's many prophetic details is fulfilled when witnesses of the crucifixion taunt Jesus as he dies: "So also the chief priests, with the scribes and elders, mocked him, saying, 'He saved others; he cannot save himself. He is the King of Israel; let him come down now from the cross, and we will believe in him. He trusts in God; let God deliver him now'" (Matt. 27:41–43).

The Suffering Servant

Isaiah 53

Who has believed what he has heard from us?
And to whom has the arm of the Lord been revealed?
For he grew up before him like a young plant,
and like a root out of dry ground;
he had no form or majesty that we should look at him,
and no beauty that we should desire him.
He was despised and rejected by men,
a man of sorrows and acquainted with grief;
and as one from whom men hide their faces
he was despised, and we esteemed him not.

Surely he has borne our griefs
and carried our sorrows;
yet we esteemed him stricken,
smitten by God, and afflicted.
But he was pierced for our transgressions;
he was crushed for our iniquities;
upon him was the chastisement that brought us peace,
and with his wounds we are healed.
All we like sheep have gone astray;
we have turned—every one—to his own way;
and the Lord has laid on him
the iniquity of us all.
He was oppressed, and he was afflicted,
yet he opened not his mouth;
like a lamb that is led to the slaughter,
and like a sheep that before its shearers is silent,
so he opened not his mouth.

By oppression and judgment he was taken away;
  and as for his generation, who considered
that he was cut off out of the land of the living,
  stricken for the transgression of my people?
And they made his grave with the wicked
  and with a rich man in his death,
although he had done no violence,
  and there was no deceit in his mouth.
Yet it was the will of the Lord to crush him;
  he has put him to grief;
when his soul makes an offering for guilt,
  he shall see his offspring; he shall prolong his days;
the will of the Lord shall prosper in his hand.

Out of the anguish of his soul he shall see and be satisfied;
by his knowledge shall the righteous one, my servant,
  make many to be accounted righteous,
  and he shall bear their iniquities.
Therefore I will divide him a portion with the many,
  and he shall divide the spoil with the strong,
because he poured out his soul to death
  and was numbered with the transgressors;
yet he bore the sin of many,
  and makes intercession for the transgressors. ■

Previous: Robert Hills, *Five Sheep*, no date

THIS MOVING POEM IS ONE of four songs of the Suffering Servant that are found in the book of Isaiah. It is a messianic prophecy about the atoning death of Jesus, and it is such a complete exposition that even the New Testament does not give us a clearer account of the atoning nature of Christ's death on the cross.

This poem is more literary than is commonly realized. One aspect of this is that it belongs to an esteemed genre known as *encomium*—a poem or prose piece that praises either a character type (such as the virtuous wife, in Proverbs 31) or an abstract quality (such as love, in 1 Corinthians 13). Certain standard features appear in an encomium: a formal introduction to the subject of its praise; the distinguished position and ancestry of the subject; a list of the superior qualities and acts of the subject; and a statement of the rewards that accompany those qualities and acts.

Isaiah 53 is a subversion of the conventional encomium. It imitates the conventions of the genre but inverts them. At the heart of this subversion is the paradox of Christ's atoning death: at a physical level it was an ignominious miscarriage of justice and a seeming defeat, but at a spiritual level it

Rene Romero Schuler, *Shadow*, 2012

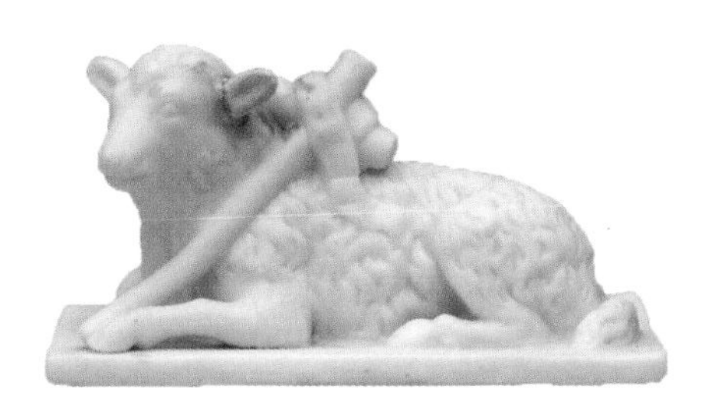

was a triumph that accomplished the salvation of many people. As in the conventional encomium, Isaiah 53 praises its subject, but it praises him for what by ordinary human standards of success are the wrong reasons.

Here are just a few ways in which the song subverts our expectations. Instead of being a heroic figure to whom the masses flock, this Suffering Servant is despised. The praiseworthy acts that he performs are ones that the human race seeks to avoid. The Suffering Servant is even condemned in a court of justice and dies a criminal's death. But after listing these unheroic acts, the poem paradoxically praises the Suffering Servant as being a conquering hero who divides the spoils after battle. The reason for this elevation of the Suffering Servant is given at the end of the poem, when we are led to contemplate what his suffering and death accomplished: the redemption of sinners through a substitutionary atonement.

One more paradox remains to be noted. The subject matter of this poem is on one level distressing: it portrays the rejection and agonizing death of an innocent man. But the poetry of the passage is the very pinnacle of verbal beauty. The poem abounds in striking imagery and metaphors, and it uses the verse form of parallelism to perfection. The aphoristic or memorable quality of the lines and phrases makes its statements almost impossible to forget. These aspects of the poem fit perfectly with the paradox at its heart, namely, an apparent defeat is actually a beautiful victory.

This poem will repay all the devotional attention that we give it. It is the clearest expression we have of certain features of Christ's atoning death, such as the sorrow we feel over his suffering and the substitutionary nature of his death that accomplished our salvation. ■

Our familiar Christological understanding of this poem of the Suffering Servant is confirmed in the story of the Ethiopian eunuch narrated in Acts 8:26–35. When the eunuch reads from this text and asks Philip whether the prophet is speaking of himself or someone else, "Philip opened his mouth, and beginning with this Scripture he told him the good news about Jesus" (v. 35). We should note that the story of the Suffering Servant is *good* news.

Lid of box, 1830–70

Even Death on a Cross

PHILIPPIANS 2:5–11

Have this mind among yourselves,
which is yours in Christ Jesus,

who, though he was in the form of God,
did not count equality with God a thing to be grasped,
but emptied himself,
by taking the form of a servant,
being born in the likeness of men.

And being found in human form,
he humbled himself
by becoming obedient to the point of death,
even death on a cross.

Therefore God has highly exalted him
and bestowed on him the name
that is above every name,

so that at the name of Jesus every knee should bow,
in heaven and on earth and under the earth,
and every tongue confess that Jesus Christ is Lord,
to the glory of God the Father. ■

THIS IS ONE OF SEVERAL famous Christ hymns found in the New Testament. The first is the prologue to John's gospel, which celebrates Christ's coming to earth. Even though it is a Christmas poem rather than a crucifixion poem, one line stands out in its relevance to Christ's passion: "He came to his own, and his own people did not receive him" (John 1:11). Another Christ hymn, found in Colossians 1:15–20, praises Christ's preeminence in the cosmos and the church, and it too refers to the crucifixion when it calls Christ "the firstborn from the dead" (v. 18).

Despite the brevity and simplicity of the Christ hymn in Philippians 2, it is as expansive as any other entry in this anthology. It begins by taking us to the decision that Milton imagined in full detail in his dialogue in heaven (see pages 24–28): the Son's decision to become an atoning sacrifice. The poem then takes us through Christ's incarnation, crucifixion, and exaltation after his resurrection.

Saints and Worshippers in Adoration, 1510/15

As we follow this sequence, we see that it is arranged in the shape of a funnel—from Christ's descent from heavenly and divine glory into human form to his further humbling as he dies on a cross. But at this point, the flow of thought and emotion pivots and soars upward. Christ is accorded an exaltation that fills our imaginations to the bursting point. This is achieved by a vocabulary of superlatives: *highly exalted*, *above every name*, *every knee*, *every tongue*. And simply to say *every knee* is not enough; the poet expands on this with the parallel phrases *in heaven and on earth and under the earth*.

The earlier poems in this unit are prospective in orientation, looking forward to the events of Holy Week. This Christ hymn is retrospective, looking back on events that have been already accomplished. Yet it has the same feel as the other poems in the sense that it leads us to see the principles underlying Christ's death and resurrection. The theological substructure of the poem and of God's redemptive plan is known as *Christ's humiliation and exaltation*. A detailed outline of the poem reveals that it unfolds according to the following topics: Christ's preexistent being; his choice, incarnation, abasement, and exaltation; universal homage to Christ; a christological confession.

In addition to prompting us to meditate on the whole story of Holy Week, this poem has a surprise twist that we should not overlook. We have a natural tendency to think of Good Friday as a defeat and Easter as a victory. On a physical level, the death of Jesus could indeed be considered a depressing defeat. But, when rightly viewed, the events of Good Friday were a victory. That is why the Christ hymn claims that Christ's death is the reason for his exaltation: Therefore *God has highly exalted him*.

This poem can serve a meditative role by leading us to contemplate the totality of Christ's redemptive mission and its reward and, in keeping with the lead-in to the hymn, to prompt us to resolve to emulate Jesus' humility and self-sacrifice. ■

Hebrews 12:2 corresponds to this passage in that it offers Jesus as our example to emulate and also encompasses both his humiliation and exaltation: Let us "[look] to Jesus, the founder and perfecter of our faith, who for the joy that was set before him endured the cross, despising the shame, and is seated at the right hand of the throne of God."

HOLY WEEK

TOWARD THE CROSS

What is known as Holy Week has the shape of a story, which, after all, it is. This story begins at a high point of euphoria on Palm Sunday, which is one of the most celebratory events in the annual Christian calendar.

Thursday evening in the upper room is a transition moment. It is filled with gracious exchanges between Jesus and his disciples, although these are conducted with references to the coming agony of Jesus. That agony reaches its point of greatest extremity at midnight in the garden of Gethsemane.

The entries in this section follow the contour of the events noted above. ■

Rodrigo de Osona the Elder,
The Agony in the Garden, ca. 1465

Psalm for Palm Sunday

SELECTIONS FROM THE OLD TESTAMENT

Prophet

Rejoice greatly, O daughter of Zion!
  Shout aloud, O daughter of Jerusalem!
Behold, your king is coming to you;
  righteous and having salvation is he,
humble and mounted on a donkey,
  on a colt, the foal of a donkey.

Psalmist

Glad songs of salvation
  are in the tents of the righteous:
"The right hand of the Lord does valiantly,
  the right hand of the Lord exalts,
  the right hand of the Lord does valiantly!"

Open to me the gates of righteousness,
  that I may enter through them.
This is the gate of the Lord;
  the righteous shall enter through it.

Blessed is he who comes in the name of the Lord!
  We bless you from the house of the Lord.

The righteous flourish like the palm tree
  and grow like a cedar in Lebanon.

The Lord

I have set my King
  on Zion, my holy hill.

David

Out of the mouth of babies and infants,
you have established strength because of your foes,
to still the enemy and the avenger.

Prophet

Of the increase of his government and of peace
there will be no end,
on the throne of David and over his kingdom,
to establish it and to uphold it
with justice and with righteousness
from this time forth and forevermore.
The zeal of the Lord of hosts will do this.

The Lord to David

I will raise up your offspring after you,
and I will establish his kingdom.
And your house and your kingdom
shall be made sure forever before you.
Your throne shall be established forever.

Prophet

Behold, God is my salvation;
I will trust, and will not be afraid;
for the Lord God is my strength and my song,
and he has become my salvation.
With joy you will draw water
from the wells of salvation.

Sing praises to the Lord, for he has done gloriously;
let this be made known in all the earth.
Shout, and sing for joy, O inhabitant of Zion,
for great in your midst is the Holy One of Israel. ■

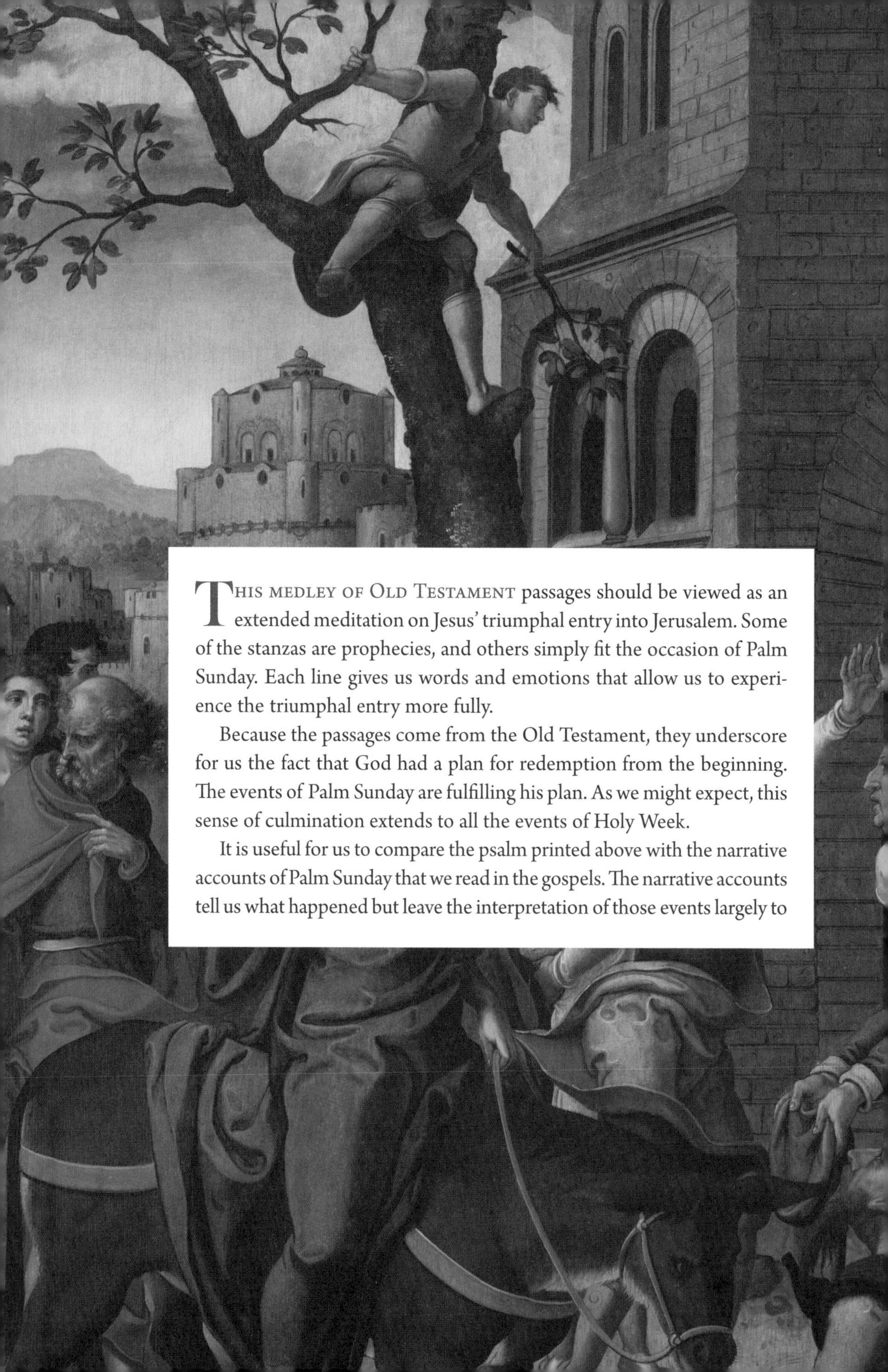

THIS MEDLEY OF OLD TESTAMENT passages should be viewed as an extended meditation on Jesus' triumphal entry into Jerusalem. Some of the stanzas are prophecies, and others simply fit the occasion of Palm Sunday. Each line gives us words and emotions that allow us to experience the triumphal entry more fully.

Because the passages come from the Old Testament, they underscore for us the fact that God had a plan for redemption from the beginning. The events of Palm Sunday are fulfilling his plan. As we might expect, this sense of culmination extends to all the events of Holy Week.

It is useful for us to compare the psalm printed above with the narrative accounts of Palm Sunday that we read in the gospels. The narrative accounts tell us what happened but leave the interpretation of those events largely to us. Additionally, the gospel stories of Palm Sunday place the events into a sequence that has a beginning, middle, and end. Poetry lacks such a logical sequence. It gives us impressionistic snapshots and jumps in disjoined fashion from one detail to another. Poetry is preeminently a *response* to something, and this Palm Sunday psalm sizzles with a series of heightened responses to Jesus' triumphal entry into Jerusalem. Above all, this psalm demonstrates appropriate emotional responses to the events of Palm Sunday, awakening them in us as well.

Since the stanzas that make up the psalm were not intended specifically to serve as an account of Palm Sunday, we need to be active in analyzing how each stanza fits some aspect of the triumphal entry. We will be aided in this if we are aware of the poetic images and literary motifs that the psalm shares with the gospel narratives of Palm Sunday. The main motifs we see are rejoicing and shouting; joy and gladness; kingship; the triumphant progression of a king into Zion, the chief city of the kingdom; entering city gates; conquest and the resultant salvation of a people; the Davidic line; God as the Holy One who is the ultimate actor in the drama. If we spend enough time unpacking these motifs and meditating on them, we will experience a heightened understanding of the triumphal entry as well as an invigorating emotional involvement in it. ■

The glue that holds this psalm together is the actual events of Palm Sunday. Here is a brief "video clip" of those events: "And the crowds that went before [Jesus] and that followed him were shouting, 'Hosanna to the son of David! Blessed is he who comes in the name of the Lord!'... And when he entered Jerusalem, the whole city was stirred up" (Matt. 21:9, 10).

Pieter Coecke van Aelst, *Entry into Jerusalem*, ca. 1530–35

All Glory, Laud, and Honor

Theodulf of Orléans (ca. 750–821)
Translated by John Mason Neale (1818–1866)

All glory, laud, and honor
To thee, Redeemer, King,
To whom the lips of children
Made sweet hosannas ring.

Thou art the King of Israel,
Thou David's royal Son,
Who in the Lord's name comest,
The King and Blessed One.

The company of angels
Are praising thee on high,
And mortal men and all things
Created make reply.

The people of the Hebrews
With palms before thee went;
Our praise and prayer and anthems
Before thee we present.

To thee, before thy passion,
They sang their hymns of praise;
To thee, now high exalted,
Our melody we raise.

Thou didst accept their praises;
Accept the prayers we bring,
Who in all good delightest,
Thou good and gracious King. ■

THIS IS THE ONE INDISPUTABLE Palm Sunday hymn of the Christian world. Originally composed in Latin in 820, it is the customary processional Palm Sunday hymn in liturgical churches and a rousing hymn sung at Palm Sunday services in nonliturgical churches. We will grasp the devotional thrust of this esteemed hymn only if we understand Palm Sunday correctly.

Although the triumphal entry of Jesus into Jerusalem marked the beginning of the events of Holy Week, we should not view Jesus' exaltation by children and the common people through a lens of suspicion. It is unlikely that the people who exalted Jesus as king on Palm Sunday were the same people who shouted "Crucify him" five days later. The celebrants at the triumphal entry got it right when they exalted Jesus as God's anointed king. They did not hold back in their exaltation, and neither should we. The triumphal entry was a preview of the exaltation of Jesus after his death and resurrection. On Palm Sunday, Jesus made a public claim to be the prophesied Messiah, and his subsequent death and resurrection validated that claim.

This hymnic poem's overall strategy is to make us participants in the events of the first Palm Sunday. For example, its opening two lines express our own praise of Christ, and the next two lines whisk our imaginations to the parallel action of the first Palm Sunday. Similarly, each of its last three stanzas is evenly divided between describing what the celebrants did on the first Palm Sunday and what *we* do.

Several genres combine within this hymnic poem. It is a song of praise that exalts Christ the way the Old Testament psalms of praise

exalt God. Its continuous references to *thee* and *thou* alert us to the fact that the poem is a prayer addressed directly to Jesus. The poem's stance is not that of an individual praise song and prayer but that of a corporate one, as embodied in the plural pronouns *we* and *our*.

As we contemplate this exalted praise song devotionally, we find our attention directed to specific theological aspects of Jesus' role as Savior. This rich vein of theological reflection is concentrated in the second stanza, which refers to Jesus as *King of Israel*, *David's royal Son*, the one who *comest* from God, and *the King and Blessed One*.

The poem's devotional takeaways keep multiplying. The poet becomes our representative who gives us the right words to express our own adoration of Jesus. We are also made aware of the unity we share with believers from all ages, and even with the angels, as we praise this worthy Savior, and we are invited to unpack the implications of the idea that Jesus is King. ■

This Palm Sunday poem is based on the gospels' narrative accounts of the triumphal entry. Here is John's:

> The next day the large crowd that had come to the feast heard that Jesus was coming to Jerusalem. So they took branches of palm trees and went out to meet him, crying out, "Hosanna! Blessed is he who comes in the name of the Lord, even the King of Israel!" (John 12:12–13)

Jan Luyken, *Entry into Jerusalem*, 1712

’Tis Midnight, and on Olive’s Brow

William B. Tappan (1794–1849)

’Tis midnight, and on Olive’s brow
The star is dimmed that lately shone;
’Tis midnight in the garden now,
The suffering Savior prays alone.

’Tis midnight, and from all removed,
The Savior wrestles lone with fears;
Even that disciple whom he loved
Heeds not his Master’s grief and tears.

’Tis midnight, and for other’s guilt
The Man of Sorrows weeps in blood;
Yet He that hath in anguish knelt
Is not forsaken by His God.

’Tis midnight, and from heavenly plains
Is borne the song that angels know;
Unheard by mortals are the strains
That sweetly soothe the Savior’s woe. ■

“’Tis Midnight” is based on the gospels’ narrative of what took place in Gethsemane before Jesus’ arrest—part of which reads as follows:

> [Jesus] knelt down and prayed, saying, “Father, if you are willing, remove this cup from me. Nevertheless, not my will, but yours, be done.” And there appeared to him an angel from heaven, strengthening him. And being in agony he prayed more earnestly; and his sweat became like great drops of blood falling down to the ground. (Luke 22:41–44)

The author of this hymnic poem was a Boston clockmaker who became a prolific poet and hymnwriter, publishing no fewer than ten volumes of poetry and hymns. When William Tappan wrote and published "'Tis Midnight" at the young age of twenty-eight, he had just become superintendent of the American Sunday School Union. The simplicity of the hymn grows out of his heart for children of the faith.

The poem recreates Christ's agony in the garden of Gethsemane. It is more descriptive than interpretive and follows a narrative sequence stanza by stanza. The first stanza composes the scene: Jesus is alone in the garden in the darkness of the night. The second stanza intensifies the loneliness of Jesus' situation and reminds us that it was an experience of *fears*, *grief*, and *tears*.

The poem becomes more complex in its third stanza. The words not only keep alive our awareness that Jesus is enduring grief and agony but also bring to our attention the fact that he is bearing the weight of the sins of the world. This is balanced by an assertion that he has not been abandoned by his Father. The final stanza ends its description of Jesus' ordeal in the garden on a note of consolation as he is soothed by a heavenly comforter.

There is just enough interpretive overlay on the poem's description of these literal events to make the work satisfying to adult understanding. To the degree to which the poem is descriptive rather than interpretive, it invites us to come to our own interpretations and applications of the events that it places before us for contemplation.

Someone who shows us how to do this is Harriet Beecher Stowe, who stresses the way in which Jesus' actions in Gethsemane can serve as a pattern for us when we are suffering as well as an assurance that he sympathizes with our griefs. Stowe observes that all people have their private Gethsemanes. It was for this reason that God "provided us with a divine Friend who had been through the deepest [sorrows] and come out victorious." Jesus "knows what it is . . . to suffer . . . ; He can understand us, and can help us. He can send an angel from heaven to comfort us when every human comforter is sleeping."

As we contemplate Jesus' agony in the garden, we come to understand him more fully and love him more ardently. ■

School of Florence, *The Agony in the Garden* (detail), 1320

Love

George Herbert (1593–1633)

Love bade me welcome: yet my soul drew back,
  Guilty of dust and sin.
But quick-eyed Love, observing me grow slack
  From my first entrance in,
Drew nearer to me, sweetly questioning
  If I lacked anything.

A guest, I answered, worthy to be here:
  Love said, You shall be he.
I the unkind, ungrateful? Ah my dear,
  I cannot look on thee.
Love took my hand, and smiling did reply,
  Who made the eyes but I?

Truth Lord, but I have marred them: let my shame
  Go where it doth deserve.
And know you not, says Love, who bore the blame?
  My dear, then I will serve.
You must sit down, says Love, and taste my meat:
  So I did sit and eat. ■

Among English devotional poets, George Herbert holds a revered place. While in college, he decided that he would write poetry only on spiritual experiences. Even though he grew up in aristocratic circumstances, he became an Anglican clergyman in a humble rural village near the cathedral town of Salisbury.

His poem "Love" has three simultaneous levels of meaning, and if we bring these into play, we see that the poem could appear in three different units of this anthology.

First, the poem concludes Herbert's volume of devotional poems titled *The Temple*, where it is preceded by the poems "Death," "Judgment," and "Heaven." In other words, "Love" is about God's welcoming a sinner into heaven, and as such it could appear in the "Raised with Christ: Life Everlasting" section of this anthology.

But God's invitation to partake of a meal is also a metaphor for his offer of salvation, which we accept at the moment of conversion, and the poem therefore could belong under the heading "Redemption Applied."

Yet the poem's third level of meaning gives it a fitting place in this particular unit, where we consider the events of Holy Week that led up to Good Friday. In some liturgical circles, this poem is known as a Maundy Thursday poem. The word *maundy* is based on the Latin word for "command" and refers to the command Jesus gave his disciples, when he instituted the Lord's Supper in the upper room, to love one another and observe the sacrament of Communion in remembrance of his death. The poem readily evokes the picture of God's love that is extended through the communion table.

What about the poem itself? It is based on a conversation between two personified beings: the speaker's soul and an attribute of God—namely, his love. The conversation is actually a debate, in which a host invites a guest to stay for a meal and the guest offers a series of objections related to his unworthiness. In addition to the literary form of the debate, the narrative motif of the quest is present, inasmuch as the divine host undertakes a quest to convince the reluctant guest to accept his invitation.

Specific Holy Week motifs enter the poem as well. The guest is reluctant to stay because of his guilt, sin, unworthiness, and shame.

Luis Meléndez, *Still Life with Figs and Bread*, ca. 1770

This describes nothing less than the sinful condition that necessitated Jesus' sacrifice. When the host asks, "Who bore the blame?" we are led to contemplate Jesus' substitutionary atonement on the cross.

By means of the poem's extended back-and-forth swing of the pendulum between human unworthiness and divine love, we are led to feel the persistence of God's love as we see that he does not allow sinners to refuse his great invitation. ■

This poem is a mosaic of biblical allusions that builds to a climax at the end. In the Bible translation Herbert would have used, Jesus describes the return of a lord, representing himself, who "shall gird himself, and make [his servants] to sit down to meat, and will come forth and serve them" (Luke 12:37 KJV).

Ugolino da Siena, *The Last Supper*, ca. 1325–30

ON THE CROSS

REDEMPTION ACCOMPLISHED

The poems in this unit contemplate the events of Good Friday. Accordingly, one thrust of the poems is to situate us at the cross. The effectiveness of the poems in this unit depends on our ability to visualize what happened on the day of Jesus' crucifixion. We will not be moved as we should if we do not vicariously join the band of Jesus' followers who stood within sight of the cross on Good Friday.

But the poems do more than awaken our imaginative presence at the cross. They also subject the physical facts of the crucifixion to analysis. At this level they activate our understanding, so we need to follow the poems' prompting to think about the physical happenings of Good Friday.

Through the threefold contemplative exercise that dates to the Middle Ages and is explained in the introduction to this anthology, elements of application, thanksgiving, and resolve emerge as well. ■

Lead Me to Calvary

Jennie Evelyn Hussey (1874–1958)

King of my life, I crown thee now,
Thine shall the glory be;
Lest I forget thy thorn crowned brow,
Lead me to Calvary.

Show me the tomb where thou wast laid,
Tenderly mourned and wept;
Angels in robes of light arrayed
Guarded thee whilst thou slept.

Let me like Mary, through the gloom,
Come with a gift to thee;
Show to me now the empty tomb,
Lead me to Calvary.

May I be willing, Lord, to bear
Daily my cross for thee;
Even thy cup of grief to share,
Thou hast borne all for me.

Refrain
Lest I forget Gethsemane,
Lest I forget thine agony;
Lest I forget thy love for me,
Lead me to Calvary. ■

THE PURPOSE OF DEVOTIONAL POEMS that focus on the cross of Christ is to lead us, in our thoughts and feelings, to Calvary. Thus this particular poem is a fitting choice to begin this section of the anthology. Its author was a Quaker who suffered from debilitating rheumatism during the last forty years of her life, during which she also cheerfully cared for her invalid sister. She wrote "Lead Me to Calvary" during Passion Week and first published it in 1921.

Thomas Moran, *Mountain of the Holy Cross*, 1890

The poem is a prayer addressed to Jesus. Opening with an invocation to Jesus as *King of my life*, it addresses Christ no fewer than a dozen times, making this a poem of intense personal devotion. Its first two lines express adoration for Jesus, embodied in (a) the exalted epithet *King of my life*, (b) a metaphoric crowning of him, and (c) an ascription of *glory* to him. The rest of the opening stanza announces the theme of the poem—the need not to forget Christ's crucifixion—accompanied by a way to ensure that we remember Christ's crucifixion: being led to Calvary.

The remaining three stanzas are a list of petitions to Jesus as we follow the lead of the poem. Within this structure, we can discern a clear progression of thought. The second stanza composes the scene of Jesus in the tomb, which is portrayed, in an idealized way, as a scene of tender mourning in which Jesus is guarded by angels in robes of light. From the closed tomb we are led in the next stanza to think about the empty tomb of Easter. In the final stanza, we move beyond Holy Week with a resolve to bear Christ's cross in our daily living. This too is a way for us not to forget Gethsemane and Calvary.

We should note in passing that biographers of Hussey record that when visitors observed her cheerful devotion to her invalid sister, she often referenced Luke 9:23, which records Jesus' statement "If anyone would come after me, let him deny himself and take up his cross daily and follow me."

The refrain casts the poem in a different light. In common usage, the conjunction *lest* introduces a fear or danger that needs to be countered, as in "He grabbed the railing lest he fall." The danger that the refrain names is the danger of forgetting the suffering of Christ. Its final line, which is unusually elevated to the status of the poem's title, tells us how such forgetfulness can be countered: by being led to Calvary through remembrance and contemplation.

The poem enacts the very thing for which it prays, as it prompts us to be led to Calvary by remembering Christ's sacrifice and by embracing it with saving faith. ■

"Lead Me to Calvary" is a prayer that we will be able to remember the sacrifice of Jesus, *lest* it be forgotten to our spiritual harm. Hebrews 12:3 is similar in substance and rhetorical form: "Consider [remember] him who endured from sinners such hostility against himself, so that you may not grow weary or fainthearted."

Alas! and Did My Savior Bleed

Isaac Watts (1674–1748)

Alas! and did my Savior bleed,
And did my Sovereign die?
Would he devote that sacred head
For sinners such as I?

Was it for crimes that I had done
He groaned upon the tree?
Amazing pity! grace unknown!
And love beyond degree!

Well might the sun in darkness hide,
And shut his glories in,
When Christ, the mighty Maker, died
For man the creature's sin.

Thus might I hide my blushing face
While his dear cross appears;
Dissolve my heart in thankfulness,
And melt mine eyes in tears.

But drops of grief can ne'er repay
The debt of love I owe;
Here, Lord, I give myself away,
'Tis all that I can do. ■

As we absorb the content and movement of this poem, we put into practice the prayer of the preceding entry that we be led to Calvary. Each of this poem's first four stanzas includes details that situate us at the scene of the crucifixion and describes the poet's appropriate reactions to them. After the poet has thus composed the scene and responded to it, he leads us in the final stanza to do what centuries of meditative practice have prescribed: reach a resolution based on our contemplation. Here our "action plan" is to give our allegiance to Christ.

The skeleton on which the speaker builds his thought process is the scene of the crucifixion as narrated in the gospels. Thus we find references to Christ's bleeding and dying on the cross, his groaning in pain, and the darkness that descended during his crucifixion. Setting the scene is a minor element within the poem, but it provides the framework for the speaker's responses.

Simon Moulijn, *Crucifixion on Rock*, 1901

The main business of the poem is the expression of feeling. The range of feelings is immense and includes pity for the suffering Christ, wonder or amazement that his agony and death actually happened, a degree of incredulity over what Christ did (and for whom), a sense of sin and unworthiness, grief, and gratitude that lead to surrender to Christ.

As we look at the poem's progression in more detail, we can discern a logic to its stanzaic arrangement. The first stanza records with wonder the fact of Christ's sacrifice on the cross. The second stanza gives the reason for that sacrifice: the sins of the human race. Stanza 3 indirectly and implicitly ascribes shame to what was done to Christ at the crucifixion, and stanza 4 carries this sense of disgrace to the speaker's feelings of personal guilt, which are accompanied by gratitude for his deliverance. The logical culmination of this movement of thought and feeling comes in the last stanza, in which we discover the only adequate way of coming to grips with the crucifixion: to give oneself to Jesus in faith.

Starting with an opening exclamation and a rhetorical question, the poem does a marvelous job of capturing the amazement and even incredulity that we rightly feel when we ponder Christ's sacrifice. The first two stanzas lead us to ask, "Is this really happening?" In the next two stanzas, the poet exclaims that if these amazing things are really happening, it is no wonder that the world is engulfed in darkness. The last stanza then unfolds a final realization—that the human grief poured forth throughout the poem cannot achieve salvation. We attain redemption only through belief in the crucified Savior. (Fanny Crosby gave her life to Jesus at a revival meeting while singing the line *Here, Lord, I give myself away*.)

As we meditate on the cross, this poem can serve to awaken godly emotions regarding Christ's sacrifice. Isaac Watts emphasized this focus with the heading or subtitle he ascribed to it when it was first published in 1707: "Godly sorrow arising from the sufferings of Christ." ■

This poem pictures the extreme suffering that Jesus underwent as he atoned for the sins of fallen people. The song of the Suffering Servant in Isaiah 53 is a parallel passage, which is examined in greater detail on pages 33–36 and excerpted here: "But he was pierced for our transgressions; he was crushed for our iniquities; upon him was the chastisement that brought us peace, and with his wounds we are healed" (v. 5).

His Savior's Words, Going to the Cross

Robert Herrick (1591–1674)

Have, have ye no regard, all ye
Who pass this way, to pity me,
Who am a man of misery!

A man both bruised and broke, and one
Who suffers not here for mine own,
But for my friends' transgression!

Ah! Sion's Daughters, do not fear
The cross, the cords, the nails, the spear,
The myrrh, the gall, the vinegar:

For Christ, your loving Savior, hath
Drunk up the wine of God's fierce wrath;
Only, there's left a little froth,

Less for to taste, than for to show,
What bitter cups had been your due,
Had He not drunk them up for you. ■

Herrick's poem is primarily about the suffering that Jesus endured in place of sinners. First Peter 2:24 covers the same territory: "He himself bore our sins in his body on the tree. . . . By his wounds you have been healed."

THE FIRST THING THAT DRAWS our attention in this poem is its apparent simplicity. It is written in three-line stanzas, and all the lines in each stanza share the same rhyming sound at the end.

In a poem full of surprise twists, perhaps the first comes in the title, which gives us Jesus' words *going to the cross* in place of his famous words *from the cross*. This is the poet's imagined speech by Jesus to his followers as he walks to his crucifixion.

Complexity lies below the simple surface we have noted. Who is speaking in the second part of the poem? Although a cursory reading might lead us to think that the shift to the third person that starts in the third stanza signals that someone other than Jesus is speaking, closer analysis makes it likely that the entire poem is spoken by Jesus. And who are the imagined *daughters* of *Sion*, or Zion, to whom Jesus speaks? This epithet is common in the Bible, and it refers most generally to all believers in God.

With these questions answered, we naturally turn our attention to the devotional content of the poem. The work's primary focus is on the sufferings that Jesus endured as he served as a sacrifice in the place of sinners. The packed third stanza reminds us of nearly every aspect of the physical torture that Jesus endured during his passion. In the stanzas before and after, Jesus himself uses a vocabulary of agony and physical pain to evoke our pity for his suffering.

The poem orchestrates the physical sensations and powerful emotions of Jesus' suffering to continuously remind us that he endured these things as a substitute for sinners. That is why the daughters of Sion are told not to fear. This is a poem of surprises, as our pity and sorrow over the spectacle of Jesus' agony are first aroused and then allayed when we are told not to fear the horror that is held before us. But just as this welcome relief settles in, the poem springs one more surprise on us. We aren't off the hook after all, according to the final stanza.

We all know that God allows suffering to enter our lives, but for what purpose? According to the last stanza, the purpose is to allow us to experience just a little of the agony Christ suffered on the cross. Even this twist is handled in an unexpected way, as the poem does not say that our suffering is designed to make us understand what happened *to Jesus* but rather focuses on what would have happened *to us* if he had not endured pain for us.

The main devotional thrust of the poem is to lead us to feel sorrow over what Jesus endured as our substitute as well as gratitude for our deliverance. ■

Claude Déruet, *Road to Calvary*, 1615/20

The Agony

George Herbert (1593–1633)

Philosophers have measured mountains,
Fathomed the depths of seas, of states, and kings,
Walked with a staff to heaven, and traced fountains:
But there are two vast, spacious things,
The which to measure it doth more behove,
Yet few there are that sound them: Sin and Love.

Who would know Sin, let him repair
Unto mount Olivet; there shall he see
A man so wrung with pains, that all his hair,
His skin, his garments bloody be.
Sin is that press and vice, which forceth pain
To hunt his cruel food through every vein.

Who knows not Love, let him assay
And taste that juice, which on the cross a pike
Did set again abroach, then let him say
If ever he did taste the like.
Love is that liquor sweet and most divine,
Which my God feels as blood; but I, as wine. ■

As do the other poems in this unit, this classic work by George Herbert contemplates what transpired at the cross during Jesus' crucifixion. Herbert's poem does not stay at the physical level of Christ's torture and agony but places on it a theological overlay by speaking of sin and divine love. Because its subject is Christ's suffering during his passion, the poem includes the agony of Gethsemane as well as the torture that led up to and throughout the crucifixion.

"The Agony" possesses a clear stanza-by-stanza topical arrangement. Its opening stanza introduces the twofold subject of the poem's meditation. This introduction is managed in such a way as to accentuate the magnitude of human sin and divine love. Human *philosophers* (scholars and deep thinkers) are credited with having uncovered the truth about the *vast* and *spacious* dimensions of the universe. But this triumph of human knowledge is only a foil that sets off, or heightens, two far greater wonders: sin and love. These two subjects are then explored respectively in the stanzas that follow.

Great literature reminds us of what we already know, but it also presents us with new angles of vision. This poem illustrates this truth to perfection. We are accustomed to think that Christ's suffering demonstrates God's love—one of the two announced subjects of this poem. But in a

Mystical Winepress from Lelów (detail), 1647

surprise twist, the second stanza of the poem claims that Christ's agony is evidence of human sin, referring not only to the sin of those who tortured Christ but to that of sinful humanity for whom Christ died. This striking idea is mentioned only briefly, however. The bulk of the stanza makes us feel the pain that Christ experienced in the garden of Gethsemane and during his torture before and throughout the crucifixion. To make his pain vivid, Herbert employs imagery of machines (*press and vice*) that squeeze juice out of plants to portray the extreme physical mutilation of Jesus' body, along with its accompanying agony.

When the third stanza turns to the second announced subject—love—here too we are in for a surprise. The imagery of physical torture from the previous stanza appears again in the mention of the *pike* that pierced Christ's body to *set abroach*, or let out, his blood. But this imagery of flowing blood is actually a setup for the poem's climactic surprise. Where do we see God's love? Given the poem's title, we are inclined to say, "In Christ's suffering and death." But the poem surprises us by answering, "In the Communion cup." The poem connects the cross and the Lord's Supper by tying together the red liquid of Christ's shed blood and the red wine (*liquor*) of Communion. The juxtaposition of those two images paints a picture of divine leniency: Christ shed his blood in agony, while we partake of the Lord's Supper in the comfort of a church.

Poets think in images. In this poem, the abstract concepts of sin and death are rendered so concretely that we experience them as physical sensations.

The poem covers a lot of territory, but the title captures its primary devotional business: to get us to think deeply and gratefully about Christ's agony. ■

As we absorb Herbert's poem, we obey the command given to us in Hebrews 12:3: "Consider him who endured from sinners such hostility against himself."

Fritz Boehmer, *Wine Jug*, ca. 1939

STANDING AT THE CROSS

RESPONSES OF THE DEVOTED HEART

Like the poems in the preceding unit, the poems in this section compose the scene of the crucifixion. Whether explicitly or implicitly, the speakers in these poems situate themselves, and therefore us, within view of the cross. But the main focus of each poem is the speaker's *inner response* to the sight of Jesus as he dies. Their stance is introspective, and the cross governs the nature of each response. The first three poems have conviction of guilt as their theme. A sense of remorse breathes through them. The final poem in the section, "O Sacred Head, Now Wounded," includes a note of contrition but is governed by feelings of thanks and devotion for what Jesus did on the cross. ■

He Bore Our Griefs

Jacob Revius (1586–1658)
Translated by Henrietta ten Harmsel (1922–2012)

No, it was not the Jews who crucified,
Nor who betrayed you in the judgment place,
Nor who, Lord Jesus, spat into your face,
Nor who with buffets struck you as you died.
No, it was not the soldiers fisted bold
Who lifted up the hammer and the nail,
Or raised the cursèd cross on Calvary's hill,
Or, gambling, tossed the dice to win your robe.
I am the one, O Lord, who brought you there,
I am the heavy cross you had to bear,
I am the rope that bound you to the tree,
The whip, the nail, the hammer, and the spear,
The blood-stained crown of thorns you had to wear:
It was my sin, alas, it was for me. ■

Rembrandt, *The Raising of the Cross* (detail), ca. 1633

In 1633, the Dutch artist Rembrandt produced a painting that on the surface seems to be a thoroughly conventional take on a common religious subject: the raising of Jesus' cross after he was nailed to it. But Rembrandt introduced something shocking into the picture when he painted himself as one of the people hoisting the cross. Surely this is one of the most unusual self-portraits in the annals of painting. In a similar way, Rembrandt's contemporary Jacob Revius, a Dutch theologian and poet, wrote this poem to claim that it was he, and not the Jews, who crucified Jesus.

Revius's poem is a confession of guilt that he addresses directly to Christ in a prayerful stance. It follows the structure of an Italian sonnet in which the first eight lines, or *octave,* are followed by a turn in the final six lines, or *sestet.* Revius' octave rehearses what is *not* true about Christ's crucifixion: the belief that the Jews were responsible for the execution. In the sestet, the octave's positive counterpart, Revius declares what *is* true about the crucifixion: the speaker is the one responsible.

The poem's effectiveness is achieved by paradox and surprise. Everyone knows that it was the Jews who conspired against Jesus and the Romans who killed him, but that is only the externality of the matter. Who was *really* responsible for the crucifixion? Jesus' death was a substitutionary death for sinners, and so every sinner for whom Christ died can be said to be the one who killed him.

Within that theological framework, the poet rehearses the details of the crucifixion as recorded in the gospels. There is a division of duties between the octave and sestet. The first eight lines are a rogues' gallery of the worst of the worst: a description of the Jews and Roman soldiers and their actions against Jesus. In the last six lines, the speaker steps forward to confess that he is the true villain of the crucifixion story, picturing himself as not even human but instead the physical instruments of Jesus' torture. The last line is the climax of the poem and states directly the basis for the speaker's claims throughout the poem: it was his sin that caused the crucifixion.

The devotional application is for us to acknowledge that the death of Jesus was caused by the sins of humanity, including ours. ■

The biblical foundation for Revius's poem is Isaiah 53, especially the opening of verse 4: "Surely he has borne our griefs and carried our sorrows."

Good Friday

CHRISTINA ROSSETTI (1830–1894)

Am I a stone and not a sheep,
That I can stand, O Christ, beneath thy cross,
To number drop by drop thy blood's slow loss,
And yet not weep?

Not so those women loved
Who with exceeding grief lamented thee;
Not so fallen Peter weeping bitterly;
Not so the thief was moved;

Not so the sun and moon
Which hid their faces in a starless sky,
A horror of great darkness at broad noon—
I, only I.

Yet give not o'er,
But seek thy sheep, true Shepherd of the flock;
Greater than Moses, turn and look once more
And smite a rock. ■

THIS IS A POEM OF personal confession and devotion in which the speaker portrays herself as being deficient in the sorrow that she knows she should experience at the foot of the cross and prays that Christ will make her an ideal follower, as he did Peter. Her themes are embodied in a mosaic of familiar biblical references.

The poem begins, as many lyric poems do, by composing a scene and situating the speaker in it. Here the speaker paints a brief picture of the crucifixion and includes herself as an onlooker. She accuses herself of being a *stone*—emotionally unmoved—instead of a *sheep*, or follower of Jesus, who is deeply affected by the scene of her Savior's suffering.

Using a technique of foil, or contrast, the speaker lists in the middle two stanzas the figures who, unlike herself, were *moved* and shaken in a manner appropriate to the horror of the crucifixion: the *women* who lamented; *Peter*, who wept when he realized that he had betrayed Jesus; the dying *thief* who responded to Jesus with repentance; and the *sun and moon* and stars that were darkened.

Jusepe de Ribera, *Penitent Saint Peter*, 1628/32

After three stanzas of self-rebuke, in the last stanza the poet turns to Jesus in prayer. Having declared herself to be a failure in the Christian walk, the speaker asks for a rescue operation. The prayer climaxes with her request that she be smitten by Christ and made submissive to him.

The poet's concluding prayer draws upon three separate biblical reference points. The first is Jesus, who as the Good Shepherd seeks and saves his lost sheep. The second is Moses, a supreme hero of the Old Testament, yet someone whom two famous New Testament passages declare to be inferior to Christ (John 1:17 and Heb. 3:1–6). The third is Peter and specifically his denial of Jesus. On that occasion, Jesus is said to have "turned and looked at Peter" (Luke 22:61), leaving Peter convicted. Further, the name *Peter* means "rock," so in the poem's last line Jesus is said to have smitten Peter—the *rock*—with his look. We also remember that when Moses smote the rock in the wilderness, it produced life-giving water.

We should pause to admire the skill with which the poet in the last stanza reintroduces the images of sheep and rock that were present in the opening stanza of self-accusation.

The poem presents us with two devotional takeaways. First, it prompts us to experience the grief that we should feel when confronted with the details of the suffering Jesus endured for our sins. The second takeaway is a reminder that to follow Jesus requires us to repent of what is deficient in us and to ask Jesus to supply what we are lacking. The poem is both a confession of sin and a plea for renewal. ■

The speaker in this poem longs to respond appropriately to the thought of Jesus on the cross. The weeping women who followed Jesus to the crucifixion are a model of such a response: "There were also many women there looking on from a distance, who had followed Jesus from Galilee, ministering to him" (Matt. 27:55).

Étienne Bobillet and Paul Mosselman,
Mourner, ca. 1453

Spit in My Face, You Jews

JOHN DONNE (1572–1631)

Spit in my face you Jews, and pierce my side,
Buffet, and scoff, scourge, and crucify me,
For I have sinned, and sinned, and only he
Who could do no iniquity hath died.
But by my death cannot be satisfied
My sins, which pass the Jews' impiety.
They killed once an inglorious man, but I
Crucify him daily, being now glorified.
Oh let me then his strange love still admire;
Kings pardon, but he bore our punishment;
And Jacob came clothed in vile harsh attire
But to supplant, and with gainful intent;
God clothed himself in vile man's flesh, that so
He might be weak enough to suffer woe. ■

THIS PACKED SONNET DEVELOPS TWO lines of thought. One is the idea that a sinless Jesus took upon himself undeserved torture and death as a sacrifice for sinners. The other is the speaker's (and our) confession of sinfulness that deserves punishment. The overall thrust of these intertwined themes moves us to marvel at the sacrifice of Jesus.

In keeping with the focus of this unit of the anthology, the poem's first two lines situate us at the scenes of Christ's torture and crucifixion. Using a technique known as *apostrophe*—a direct address to a person who is absent but by poetic license is treated as though present and capable of responding—the speaker begins by commanding the Jews who crucified Jesus to direct their cruelty against him instead. The vividness of the

Govert Flinck, *Isaac Blessing Jacob*, ca. 1638

poet's descriptive technique leads us to ponder and recoil from the torture that was inflicted on Jesus during his passion.

What is the rationale behind the speaker's strange request to be tortured by the Jews who crucified Jesus? Lines 3 and 4 answer this question: the speaker, and we along with him, deserve punishment for our sins. But then a sudden thought intrudes (lines 5–6): our own deaths cannot atone for our sins, because they are far too great. How great are our sins? Even greater than those of the Jews who crucified Jesus (lines 6–8).

In keeping with the format of the Italian sonnet, the first eight lines, or *octave*, of this poem pose a problem: human sinfulness deserves death. The concluding six lines, or *sestet*, provide a solution to the problem: the sacrifice that the incarnate Jesus offered for the sins of the world. Donne's innovative twist of mind similarly leads us to ponder the incarnation in a new way, as he goes on to marvel at (*admire*) Christ's extraordinary (*strange*) love.

The meditation of the final lines develops two contrasts. One is between kings, who pardon with a mere declaration, and Jesus, who *bore our punishment* through his own death (line 11). The other contrast is between the patriarch Jacob and the incarnate Jesus. Both Jacob and Jesus took on *vile* clothing (in Jesus' case, the metaphoric clothing of human flesh), but they did so for opposite reasons—Jacob to deceive his father Isaac for personal benefit and Jesus to provide a sacrifice for the sins of the world. The paradoxical last line, with its assertion that God became weak, sums up the poem by jolting us into an awareness of how the substitutionary death of Jesus defies all expectation.

The devotional purpose of this poem is to move us to astonishment and gratitude as we consider that Jesus bore the punishment that we deserve. ■

Second Corinthians 5:21 encapsulates the same wonder that Donne's sonnet explores at greater length: "For our sake he made him to be sin who knew no sin, so that in him we might become the righteousness of God."

O Sacred Head, Now Wounded

Translated by Paul Gerhardt (1607–1676)
Translated by James W. Alexander (1804–1859)

O sacred Head, now wounded,
With grief and shame weighed down;
Now scornfully surrounded
With thorns, thine only crown;
O sacred Head, what glory,
What bliss till now was thine!
Yet, though despised and gory,
I joy to call thee mine.

What thou, my Lord, hast suffered
Was all for sinners' gain:
Mine, mine was the transgression,
But thine the deadly pain.
Lo, here I fall, my Savior!
'Tis I deserve thy place;
Look on me with thy favor,
Vouchsafe to me thy grace.

What language shall I borrow
To thank thee, dearest Friend,
For this thy dying sorrow,
Thy pity without end?
O make me thine forever;
And should I fainting be,
Lord, let me never, never
Outlive my love to thee.

Be near when I am dying,
O show thy cross to me;
And for my succor flying,
Come, Lord, to set me free:
These eyes, new faith receiving,
From Jesus shall not move;
For he who dies believing,
Dies safely, through thy love. ■

Victor-François-Eloi Biennourry,
The Mocking of Christ, 1852

THE MEDIEVAL POEM ON WHICH this work is based contemplated seven individual parts of the body of Jesus as he hung on the cross. Paul Gerhardt, a seventeenth-century German theologian and hymn writer, translated the poem and reworked its last movement, devoted to Christ's face, into the words of "O Sacred Head, Now Wounded." His entire poem is a prayer addressed to Jesus, and its keynote is intense personal devotion to the Savior.

The poem captures the thoughts and feelings that arise in the speaker as he imagines standing in sight of the cross. The first stanza contemplates Jesus' *Head*, which is *now wounded* and *gory*. The next stanza mentions his *deadly pain*. The third stanza keeps the cross in view by referencing his *dying sorrow*, and the final stanza asks Jesus to *show [his] cross* to the speaker when he dies, so he can receive *new faith* in his final extremity.

The responses to the crucifixion recorded in this poem are not arranged in a stanza-by-stanza topical manner; instead, they are organized in a fluid style that modern literature has taught us to call *stream of consciousness.* This means that thoughts, feelings, and ideas follow the associations that the mind somewhat randomly produces. We thus need to be alert to the following main themes of the poem and notice them whenever they appear: (1) grief over what Christ endured; (2) wonder at the magnitude of what he did for sinners; (3) gratitude to him for his sacrifice; (4) desire, expressed in a series of petitions, that Jesus will supply what we need throughout our journey of life and death; and (5) personal devotion to Jesus. As these intertwined motifs unfold, we become aware of how much the poem packs into four stanzas. The effect is that the speaker has so much to express that topically arranging it all into stanzas would be confining.

It is perhaps a slight surprise that such a mystical poem would be so theologically laden. Its four successive stanzas speak, in shorthand manner, of Christ's preincarnate existence in heaven, substitutionary atonement, pity for lost humanity, and granting of eternal life to those who believe.

Poetry depends on certain poetic conventions to achieve its effects. This poem not only expresses, but even creates, emotion through four instances of what is called the *vocative O*, a rhetorical device that elevates an utterance and expresses emotion. Its use of the exclamation *Lo* has the similar effect of drawing attention to an amazing event.

Pondering this poem leads us to feel gratitude for what Christ has done for us and to express a desire to be united to him. ■

This poem follows a rhythm in which the poet rehearses what Christ has done on behalf of believers and then resolves to claim the benefits of those acts. Psalm 116:12–13 follows a similar rhythm:

> What shall I render to the Lord
> for all his benefits to me?
> I will lift up the cup of salvation
> and call on the name of the Lord.

CLAIMING THE CROSS

REDEMPTION APPLIED

The paradigm set forth in John Murray's classic book *Redemption Accomplished and Applied* is the right one for this anthology. An earlier unit, On the Cross, focused our gaze on how Jesus' death on the cross achieved salvation for sinners. Its theme, and subtitle, is *redemption accomplished*.

This unit contains poems that describe and celebrate the redemption that results whenever a soul claims the salvation that Jesus' sacrifice accomplished on the cross. We can think of this exchange as *redemption applied*.

Because this is an anthology about the cross, the poems in this unit are not simply about the salvation we receive. They deal specifically with the basis of that salvation: Christ's shed blood and his death on the cross. ■

Redemption

George Herbert (1593–1633)

Having been tenant long to a rich Lord,
Not thriving, I resolved to be bold
And make a suit unto him, to afford
A new small-rented lease, and cancel the old.
In heaven at his manor I him sought;
They told me there that he was lately gone
About some land which he had dearly bought
Long since on earth, to take possession.
I straight returned, and knowing his great birth,
Sought him accordingly in great resorts,
In cities, theaters, gardens, parks, and courts.
At length I heard a ragged noise and mirth
Of thieves and murderers; there I him espied,
Who straight, "Your suit is granted," said, and died. ■

THE SUBJECT OF THIS SONNET is announced in its title: it is about the redemption of the human soul. This redemption is presented not as a doctrine but as an experience. The poem traces the steps by which the ordinary person can come to salvation. Although the speaker in the poem undertakes an active quest to find redemption, the poem is not primarily about this human effort. The main subject of the poem is the sacrifice of Jesus that makes salvation possible.

The poem is constructed as a narrative, as the speaker pursues a series of false leads on his quest to find a remedy for his condition. The controlling metaphor is the lord-tenant relationship. The speaker identifies himself from the start as a tenant farmer who is *not thriving* under his current rental arrangement. He therefore decides to find his *rich Lord* and ask (*make a suit unto*) him to grant him a lower-rent (*small-rented*) lease and to *cancel the old* lease. This language is of course metaphoric for the lost state (*the old*) and the redeemed, or *new*, life.

Jacopo Bassano, *The Mocking of Christ*, 1568

How can new life in Christ be attained? The poem depicts the false assumptions that the human race perennially makes in this regard. Seeking for Christ in heaven (metaphorically portrayed here as an English *manor* house) is a dead end because the rich lord is not there but on earth, an allusion to the incarnation of Jesus. The language in the middle of the poem is based on the distinction between redemption accomplished and redemption applied. The Lord *dearly bought* some land long ago at Calvary; he *take[s] possession* of it whenever someone comes to believe in him as Savior.

Learning that his lord is not in the manor, the tenant farmer next incorrectly assumes that he will be found in aristocratic earthly places of privilege. The last three lines of the poem transport our imaginations to the scene of Christ's crucifixion, as the speaker instead discovers his lord at a place of *thieves and murderers*, an execution site where he is being derided by onlookers. The speaker attains what he has sought when his lord declares his suit granted just before he dies. By means of this allusion to the crucifixion, the speaker, and we along with him, become the dying thief whose request for salvation was granted when Jesus said, "Today you will be with me in paradise" (Luke 23:43). The story that the poem tells thus uses the time-honored technique of a surprise ending.

The poem is based on the principle of reversed expectations; it presents a series of false assumptions that become discredited as the speaker's quest unfolds. As we absorb this, we are led to see with increased clarity that our redemption is a divine mystery that defies human explanation. This insight can serve as our devotional takeaway from the poem. ■

The paradox underlying "Redemption" revolves around a rich Lord who not only becomes poor but in fact dies as a sacrifice. The poem's themes bring 2 Corinthians 8:9 readily to mind: "You know the grace of our Lord Jesus Christ, that though he was rich, yet for your sake he became poor, so that you by his poverty might become rich."

Constantijn van Renesse, *The Descent from the Cross*, 1650/52

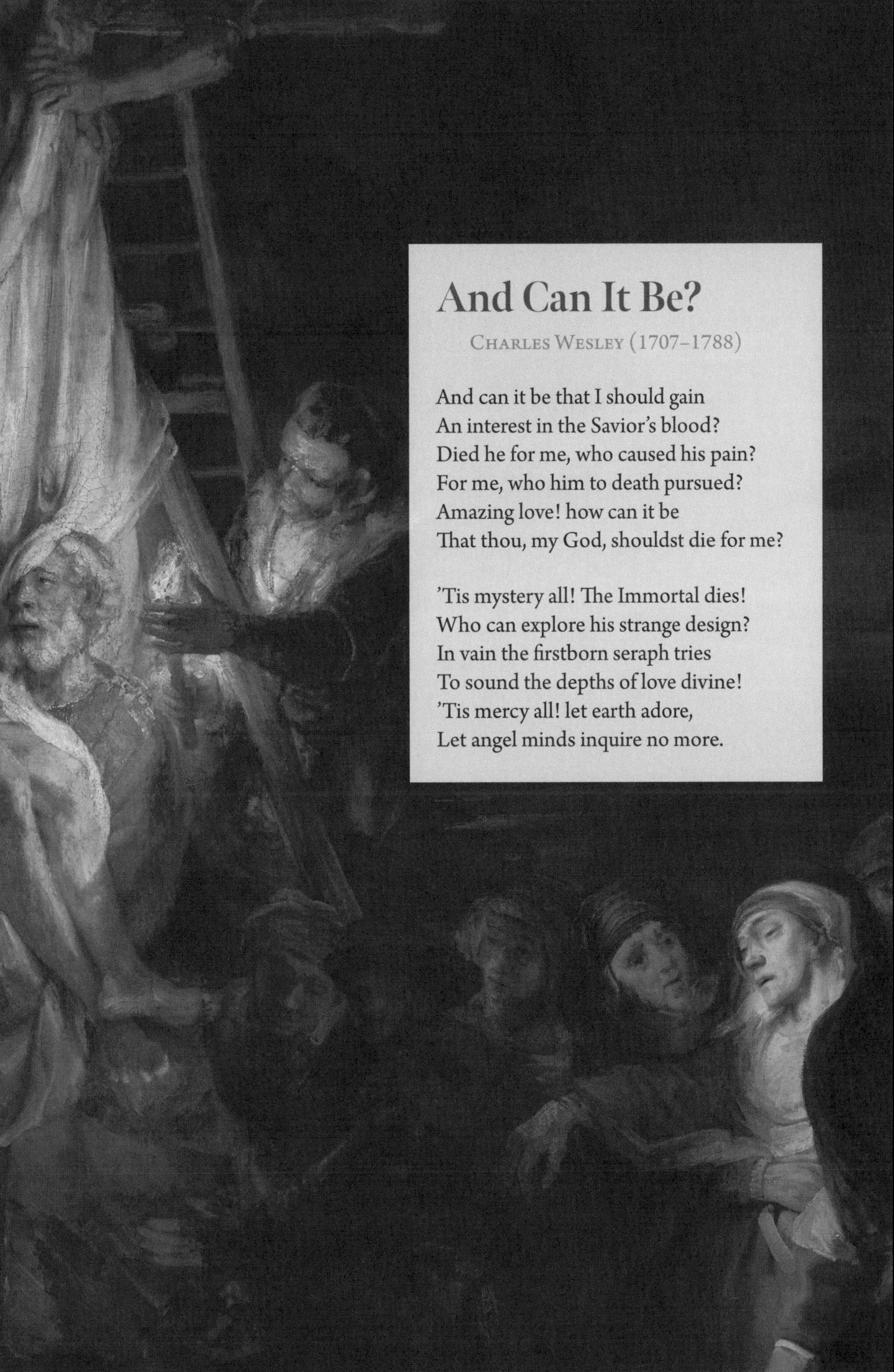

And Can It Be?

Charles Wesley (1707–1788)

And can it be that I should gain
An interest in the Savior's blood?
Died he for me, who caused his pain?
For me, who him to death pursued?
Amazing love! how can it be
That thou, my God, shouldst die for me?

'Tis mystery all! The Immortal dies!
Who can explore his strange design?
In vain the firstborn seraph tries
To sound the depths of love divine!
'Tis mercy all! let earth adore,
Let angel minds inquire no more.

He left his Father's throne above,
So free, so infinite his grace;
Emptied himself of all but love,
And bled for Adam's helpless race:
'Tis mercy all, immense and free;
For, O my God, it found out me.

Long my imprisoned spirit lay
Fast bound in sin and nature's night;
Thine eye diffused a quickening ray,
I woke, the dungeon flamed with light;
My chains fell off, my heart was free,
I rose, went forth, and followed thee.

No condemnation now I dread;
Jesus, and all in him, is mine!
Alive in him, my living head,
And clothed in righteousness divine,
Bold I approach the eternal throne,
And claim the crown, through Christ my own. ■

THIS ECSTATIC POEM RECORDS THE amazement that the redeemed soul feels upon realizing that its redemption has been not only accomplished but also personally applied. The poem does a marvelous job of capturing the universal human feeling that something has happened that seems too good to be true—and yet *is* true. The poem combines amazed acceptance and celebration of that "too good to be true" experience.

The best game plan for assimilating the poem is to progress through it stanza by stanza. The keynote of the opening stanza—a feeling of amazement—is encapsulated by its exclamation *Amazing love!* The four questions asked in this stanza are used rhetorically to express amazement bordering on incredulity—a point that the poet drives home with the nearly identical

Jacopo di Cione, *Saint Peter Released from Prison*, 1370–71

formulas *Can it be?* and *How can it be?* The sense of amazement in this stanza centers not on the atoning death of Christ as an objective reality but rather on the fact that it was *for me*, a phrase that appears three times and probably grows out of Charles Wesley's reading of Martin Luther's commentary on Galatians at the time he composed the poem.

The poem's emotional tone and exclamatory mode carry forward into its second stanza with the interjections *'Tis mystery all!* and *'Tis mercy all!* The stanza is built around a narrative thread in which the poet imagines angels attempting to explore God's love but admitting defeat. Its opening line, moreover, delivers the bold paradox of *the Immortal* Christ dying at the crucifixion.

Knowing that a feeling of ecstasy cannot be maintained indefinitely, the poet leaves his exclamatory rhetoric to give us two narrative stanzas. Stanza 3 tells the story of Christ's incarnation and atoning death. The fourth stanza narrates the conversion of the speaker (an Everyman and Everywoman figure) by telling the story from Acts 12:6–11 of Peter's rescue from prison by an angel and transforming it into a metaphoric account of personal conversion. Poetry cannot be more electrifying than this stanza is.

The concluding stanza represents the familiar eschatological turn of many hymns, as the speaker shifts his focus to the future and celebrates a heavenly existence that union with Christ has made possible. Every line in this poem can be related to familiar Bible verses; perhaps the most obvious one is this stanza's line *No condemnation now I dread*, which echoes Romans 8:1: "There is therefore now no condemnation for those who are in Christ Jesus."

English poet William Wordsworth claimed that lyric poetry corrects our feelings and gives us new compositions of feeling. We can read and reread this poem as one that expresses the feelings we should experience in response to our participation in God's great plan of redemption. ■

The sentiment of "And Can It Be?" is that salvation is too amazing to be fully understood. This finds a parallel in Ephesians 3:17–19, in which the apostle Paul prays "that Christ may dwell in your hearts through faith—that you . . . may have strength to comprehend with all the saints what is the breadth and length and height and depth, and to know the love of Christ that surpasses knowledge."

There Is a Fountain Filled with Blood

William Cowper (1731–1800)

There is a fountain filled with blood
Drawn from Emmanuel's veins;
And sinners, plunged beneath that flood,
Lose all their guilty stains.

The dying thief rejoiced to see
That fountain in his day,
And there have I, as vile as he,
Washed all my sins away.

Dear dying Lamb, thy precious blood
Shall never lose its power,
Till all the ransomed church of God
Be saved, to sin no more.

E'er since, by faith, I saw the stream
Thy flowing wounds supply,
Redeeming love has been my theme,
And shall be till I die.

When this poor lisping stammering tongue
Lies silent in the grave,
Then in a nobler sweeter song
I'll sing thy power to save. ■

Alphonse Legros, *Choir of a Spanish Church*, no date

THIS HYMNIC POEM HAS BEEN reproduced in more than two thousand hymnals since William Cowper first composed it in the late 1700s. Some are quick to assume that a hymn widely known by the masses must be simplistic and perhaps sentimental, but in fact this poem requires our best analytic effort if we are to see all that is going on in it.

At the heart of the poem is a difficult paradox that takes us to a mystical level. It is the paradox of blood that washes objects clean. First John 1:7 claims that "the blood of Jesus . . . cleanses us from all sin." Revelation 7:14 similarly speaks of saints in heaven who "have washed their robes and made them white in the blood of the Lamb." This is the paradox with which William Cowper works in this poem. When the poem speaks of blood, it refers to Jesus' sacrificial death on the cross that secured forgiveness of sins. When we come to the vocabulary of *flood*, *fountain*, *washed*, and *stream*, we need to think of water that washes clean.

A word about poetic imagery is helpful at this point. Some poetic imagery is visual, but much of it secures its effects by nonvisual means. When we encounter the metaphor of God as Father, we do not visualize him as an actual father. Instead, the qualities of fatherhood control our interpretation of this image. Similarly, when we read in the poem's opening line about a fountain filled with blood, we should not picture a bloodbath. Instead, we need to analyze the qualities of a fountain that make it an apt picture of Christ's sacrifice. A fountain perpetually pours forth an abundant flow. To *[plunge] beneath that flood* means to embrace it fully and with abandon. The poem is not intended to give us a visual tour but to lead us to contemplate

Gospel leaf depicting the Fountain of Life, first half 14th century the qualities that characterize full-hearted commitment to the sacrifice Jesus has made for the forgiveness of sins.

With these ground rules about imagery in place, we can turn to the devotional message of the poem. Most poems and hymns announce in their first line or two the theme that will control what is to follow. This poem reverses the order and uses its concluding line to summarize its content. This poem *sings*—declares and celebrates with total abandon—God's *power to save*. The title that was attached to the hymn when it was first published, "Praise for the Fountain Opened," is identical to the hymn in import: from start to finish, this poem praises the fountain of Christ's forgiveness.

A key way in which the poem develops its theme is by surveying those who are washed clean: *sinners* universally (stanza 1); the *dying thief*, who was saved on the cross (stanza 2); *the ransomed church of God*—that is, all believers (stanza 3); and the speaker as an individual believer (stanza 4).

This exuberant, overflowing poem yields more and more riches the longer we stare at it. It fits perfectly with the theme of this unit of the anthology: redemption applied—that is, embraced in personal belief. ■

When this poem was first published as a hymn, it was linked by its accompanying headnote to Zechariah 13:1: "On that day there shall be a fountain opened for the house of David and the inhabitants of Jerusalem, to cleanse them from sin and uncleanness."

Mätre Krestos, Crucifixion from the Ethiopian Gospels, early 14th century

When Rising from the Bed of Death

Joseph Addison (1672–1719)

When, rising from the bed of death,
O'erwhelmed with guilt and fear,
I see my Maker face to face,
O how shall I appear?

If yet, while pardon may be found,
And mercy may be sought,
My heart with inward horror shrinks,
And trembles at the thought;

When thou, O Lord, shalt stand disclosed
In majesty severe,
And sit in judgment on my soul,
O how shall I appear?

But thou hast told the troubled mind
Who does her sins lament,
The timely tribute of her tears
Shall endless woes prevent.

Then see the sorrow of my heart,
Ere yet it be too late,
And hear my Savior's dying groans,
To give these sorrows weight.

For never shall my soul despair
Her pardon to procure,
Who knows thine only Son has died
To make her pardon sure. ■

Hebrews 9:27–28 provides a summary statement for Addison's poem: "As it is appointed for man to die once, and after that comes judgment, so Christ . . . [has] been offered once to bear the sins of many."

We sometimes refer to the point "where the rubber meets the road." This metaphor denotes the place where theory is put to the test to determine whether it really works. The testing place for one's faith in Jesus' substitutionary atonement is before the judgment seat of God.

This is the crux of Joseph Addison's poem. It begins with a picture of the speaker rising from his deathbed and meeting his Maker face to face. The question *O how shall I appear?* means "How will God assess my spiritual condition and determine my eternal destiny? Will I stand acquitted before God the Judge?"

Addison wrote his poem during an illness that prompted the thoughts that the poem records. The only way for a meditation on Christ's atonement for our sins to avoid glibness or shallowness is for it to confront the terror of our lost state without Christ and to lead us to repent of our sins as a prerequisite for receiving forgiveness. This is where Addison's poem serves us well.

After its opening stanza composes the scene of standing before God's judgment seat, the next two stanzas give expression to the terror that we should feel when we consider our sins. The next stage of the poem, covered in the fourth and fifth stanzas, is not an easy leap to Christ's forgiveness but rather the necessary step of expressing sorrow for our sins and repenting of them. The rubber meets the road in the final stanza, as we claim the death of Christ on the cross as the basis of our pardon.

As we cast a retrospective look at the sequence we have just outlined, some further features of the poem fall into place. It has a narrative thread in which the storyline is the speaker's quest to stand acquitted before God. The stages by which the quest unfolds correspond with what theologians call the order of salvation, which starts with conviction of sin and progresses through repentance to faith in Christ's death as the means of salvation. The poem's vocabulary likewise taps into simple, bedrock Christianity: *guilt and fear* while experiencing conviction of sin, *sorrow of my heart* leading to repentance, and *my Savior's dying groans* as well as a reference to how God's *only Son has died* to indicate Christ's atoning death on the cross. The poem is nothing less than a primer on the doctrines of sin and salvation, which have been encapsulated in a dying penitent's meditation.

The specific contribution that this poem can make to our devotions is that of prompting us to take seriously the fact that "we must all appear before the judgment seat of Christ" (2 Cor. 5:10) and, in response to that awareness, to confirm our repentance and our faith in Christ's sacrifice. ■

Viktor Mikhaylovich Vasnetsov, *The Last Judgment* (details), 1885–96

Jesus, Thy Blood and Righteousness

Nicolaus L. von Zinzendorf (1700–1760)
Translated by John Wesley (1703–1791)

Jesus, thy blood and righteousness
My beauty are, my glorious dress;
'Midst flaming worlds, in these arrayed
With joy shall I lift up my head.

Bold shall I stand in that great day,
For who aught to my charge shall lay?
Fully through these absolved I am,
From sin and fear, from guilt and shame.

Lord, I believe thy precious blood,
Which, at the mercy seat of God,
Forever doth for sinners plead,
For me, e'en for my soul was shed.

Lord, I believe were sinners more
Than sands upon the ocean shore,
Thou hast for all a ransom paid,
For all a full atonement made.

When from the dust of death I rise
To claim my mansion in the skies,
Even then this shall be all my plea,
Jesus hath lived, hath died, for me.

Jesus, be endless praise to thee,
Whose boundless mercy hath for me—
For me a full atonement made,
An everlasting ransom paid. ■

PREVIOUS ENTRIES IN THIS UNIT have expressed faith in Christ's atonement and reflected on its various dimensions. "Jesus, Thy Blood and Righteousness," which was originally thirty-three stanzas long, allows us to feel what it is like to believe in the efficacy of Christ's blood to secure pardon for our sins. Our sense of having gotten inside the speaker's experience is partly secured by the first-person format of the poem. The pronouns *I*, *my*, and *me* appear seventeen times, and the assertion that the atonement is *for me* occurs three times.

The first two lines of the poem are in effect a thesis statement that controls everything that follows, while the final two lines serve as a summary.

Giovanni Baronzio, *The Baptism of Christ*, ca. 1335

As we continue to look at the poem's organization, we see that its first, last, and two middle stanzas begin with a direct address to either *Jesus* or *Lord*, making them a prayer. To this symmetry we can add a further unifying element: every stanza declares the complete efficacy of Christ's substitutionary atonement for sinners.

The poem has a strongly repetitive cast instead of a progressive one. This relieves us of searching for a topical sequence, and we can instead absorb each stanza individually as it relates to the central idea of the complete efficacy of Christ's atonement. The middle two stanzas begin with the identical clause *Lord, I believe*, giving them the quality of a formal creed or statement of belief. Taking our cue from that, we can see that the poem as a whole belongs to the genre of the charter—a declaration of the rights and privileges that belong to members of a group. As we read through the successive stanzas of this poem, we learn more and more about what we possess by virtue of belonging to the assembly of believers.

The fervor that breathes through the poem receives added depth of field if we relate it to the author's life. Nicolaus von Zinzendorf is particularly identified with a pietist group known as the Moravians, who lived on his estate. As a nineteen-year-old, Zinzendorf had the direction of his spiritual life permanently reset when he visited an art gallery in Dusseldorf, Germany, and saw a painting of Jesus being crowned with thorns. It is no wonder that he writes about Christ's atoning death with such strong personal devotion. An emphasis on religion of the heart was important not only to the Moravians but also to the later Methodist movement, and we can note that the translator of this familiar version of the poem is not, as we might expect, the hymn writer Charles Wesley but rather his brother John, whose preaching has the same *for me* emphasis as this hymn.

Acting as our representatives, poets say what we too wish to say, only they say it better. We can absorb the first-person declarations in this poem as expressions of what is in our own hearts regarding our assurance of Christ's atonement for us. ■

Romans 8:33–34 rings out the same challenge as Zinzendorf's hymn:

> Who shall bring any charge against God's elect? It is God who justifies. Who is to condemn? Christ Jesus is the one who died—more than that, who was raised—who is at the right hand of God, who indeed is interceding for us.

NEAR THE CROSS

LIFE WITH THE CROSS AT THE CENTER

Earlier units within this anthology are devoted to what happened *on the cross* and to perspectives of *standing at the cross* and *claiming the cross* through personal belief. This unit explores life *near the cross.*

The poems of this unit do not use the metaphor of living *near* or *beneath* the cross to mean picturing oneself at the crucifixion. Instead, this metaphor refers to the perspective with which a Christian lives hundreds of years after the crucifixion. The poems themselves give us an ever-expanding vision of what a cross-centered life looks like.

One thing that these poems on the aftermath of Good Friday share with the poems in the previous units is a strong sense of personal devotion to Jesus in response to his sacrifice on the cross. As we read these expressions of devotion to the cross, we need to keep in mind that the poets are not venerating the physical cross but rather writing about what was transacted on that cross. ■

Beneath the Cross of Jesus

Elizabeth Clephane (1830–1869)

Beneath the cross of Jesus
I fain would take my stand,
The shadow of a mighty rock
Within a weary land;
A home within the wilderness,
A rest upon the way,
From the burning of the noontide heat,
And the burden of the day.

Upon the cross of Jesus
Mine eye at times can see
The very dying form of One
Who suffered there for me:
And from my stricken heart with tears
Two wonders I confess,
The wonders of redeeming love
And my own worthlessness.

I take, O cross, thy shadow
For my abiding-place:
I ask no other sunshine than
The sunshine of his face;
Content to let the world go by,
To know no gain nor loss;
My sinful self my only shame,
My glory, all the cross. ■

THIS HYMNIC POEM COMBINES TWO main ideas in an easily graspable format based on a principle of contrast. We can think of these two themes as A and B. The opening stanza is devoted to theme A, which views the cross and what it represents as an overwhelming *comfort* to the believing soul. The second stanza counters this note of comfort with theme B: the cross is something that *convicts* us. The final stanza combines these two themes: its first four lines return to the theme that the cross is a comforting abiding place, and its concluding four lines again awaken the sense of human sinfulness and shame we feel when we view the glory of the cross. The effect is to make the cross a refuge from what is unbearable.

The emphasis throughout the poem is on the speaker's response to the cross. One such response is a positive embrace of the cross, as the speaker lays enthusiastic claim to all that it offers. This motion that her soul takes *toward* this desired object is balanced by a motion *away* from her sinful self, which she repudiates.

Poets speak a language of images, and many of them are the recurrent master images of life known as archetypes. This poem illustrates this to

Juan de Flandes, *Crucifixion*, ca. 1490
Following pages: Alphonse Legros, *At the Foot of the Cross*, no date

perfection. The poet lists some of the most evocative archetypes of comfort that we know—a *shadow* and *mighty rock* that protect from sun and heat, a *home*, a place of *rest*, a safe *abiding-place*, and *sunshine*. To render these pictures even more emotionally laden than they are in themselves, the poet contrasts them with unideal archetypes that are equally evocative—a *weary land*, a *wilderness*, a toilsome journey, *burning noontide heat*, and an unspecified *burden of the day*. It is impossible for poetry to carry more emotional weight than this.

To our surprise, the writer of this meditation on the meaning of the cross reaches into the Old Testament (KJV) for many of the poem's images: "the shadow of a great rock in a weary land" (Isa. 32:2); "oh that I had in the wilderness a lodging place of wayfaring men" (Jer. 9:2); "this is the rest wherewith ye may cause the weary to rest" (Isa. 28:12); "for a shadow in the day time from the heat, and for a place of refuge" (Isa. 4:6).

Our takeaway from this poem is that we need to embrace the cross as our last, best hope. ■

In this hymnic poem, the speaker places herself beneath the cross and finds worth in the cross alone. Philippians 3:7–8 expresses a similar motion of the soul: "But whatever gain I had, I counted as loss for the sake of Christ. Indeed, I count everything as loss because of the surpassing worth of knowing Christ Jesus my Lord."

When I Survey the Wondrous Cross

Isaac Watts (1674–1748)

When I survey the wondrous cross
On which the Prince of glory died,
My richest gain I count but loss,
And pour contempt on all my pride.

Forbid it, Lord, that I should boast
Save in the death of Christ my God:
All the vain things that charm me most,
I sacrifice them to his blood.

See, from his head, his hands, his feet,
Sorrow and love flow mingled down:
Did e'er such love and sorrow meet,
Or thorns compose so rich a crown?

Were the whole realm of nature mine,
That were a present far too small;
Love so amazing, so divine,
Demands my soul, my life, my all. ■

THE ESSENTIAL FEATURE OF THIS poem is signaled in its opening line. To *survey the cross* means to contemplate it, think about it, draw conclusions about it, and respond to it. This hymnic poem does all these things, with its emphasis falling on personal response and commitment. Analysis shows that the entire poem is constructed on the principle of two-line units of thought or feeling. As we assimilate the poem, therefore, we should devote attention to each pair of lines individually.

The poem is also organized on the rhetorical principle of comparison. In each stanza, the cross of Jesus is compared to something else and declared to be superior. The theme of the poem is thus the *surpassing greatness of the cross*. In successive stanzas, the cross is said to surpass the *richest gain* that we possess (stanza 1), all human things that *charm* us or claim our loyalty (stanza 2), all other displays of love and sorrow (stanza 3), and *the whole realm of nature* (stanza 4).

Mourners and Soldiers from a Crucifixion,
late 15th century

Intermingled with the theme of the surpassing wonder of the cross is a renunciation of all lesser things. In fact, when the hymn was first published, it bore the evocative heading "Crucifixion to the World by the Cross of Christ." That is what the poem is about.

The technique of "substitute naming," in which one thing is identified with something closely tied to it, is called *metonymy*. Christian poets through the centuries have said much about the cross of Christ as a way of speaking about the atonement and triumph that Jesus achieved through his death on that cross. Thus we need to understand that the poem is exalting not the physical cross but the atonement.

Each of the stanzas of this poem contributes its part to the speaker's meditation. The first two lines compose the scene. The next two lines state the first thought that the scene of Christ on the cross elicits from us: a realization that our most treasured successes are worthless when compared to the cross. The second stanza takes this thought a step further, as the speaker sacrifices his most treasured possessions to Christ's blood (another metonymy, using Christ's *blood* to mean the salvation that Christ achieved).

The third stanza paints a picture of the physical horror of the crucifixion, followed by a response to it that asserts the unparalleled nature of love and sorrow that converged in Christ's death on the cross. The final stanza recapitulates the main argument of the poem: even the best that earth offers cannot compare to the magnitude of what occurred at the cross. The poem's climax comes in its final two lines, in which the speaker commits his soul, life, and all to Christ.

The devotional goal of his poem is to prompt us to do what the speaker in the poem does: to ponder deeply what the cross means for our lives. ■

When this hymn was first published, it was accompanied by a reference to Galatians 6:14, which reads, "Far be it from me to boast except in the cross of our Lord Jesus Christ, by which the world has been crucified to me, and I to the world."

Totoya Hokkei, *A Mountainous Landscape with a Stream*, 1827

Jesus, Keep Me Near the Cross

FANNY CROSBY (1820–1915)

Jesus, keep me near the cross;
There a precious fountain,
Free to all—a healing stream—
Flows from Calvary's mountain.

Near the cross, a trembling soul,
Love and mercy found me;
There the bright and morning star
Shed its beams around me.

Near the cross! O Lamb of God,
Bring its scenes before me;
Help me walk from day to day
With its shadow o'er me.

Near the cross I'll watch and wait,
Hoping, trusting ever,
Till I reach the golden strand
Just beyond the river.

Refrain
In the cross, in the cross,
Be my glory ever;
Till my raptured soul shall find
Rest beyond the river. ■

EVEN THOUGH THE SELECTIONS IN this unit do not lead us to imagine ourselves present at the crucifixion the same way poems in earlier units do, the authors of these selections nonetheless use the same vocabulary of location. They speak of being *near* the cross or *beneath* it or in a position to *survey* it. We are to understand this metaphorically or symbolically: to be close to the cross is to keep it at the center of our thinking, feeling, and allegiance.

Fanny Crosby's famous hymn is completely controlled by the motif of being *near the cross*. In its first stanza, this formula appears as part of a petition: *Jesus, keep me near the cross*. After that, the phrase occurs at the beginning of each stanza, anchoring the speaker's entire meditation.

Poems are unified according to the principle of theme and variation. In this poem, the variations on the central theme of living close to the cross proceed in a stanza-by-stanza arrangement. The opening stanza develops the image of Christ's blood flowing as a healing stream from a fountain. Further angles of vision on the stanza emerge as we look closely at its individual images. The value of the cross is designated by the adjective *precious*. The nature of the redemption that the cross offers is that it is *free to all*. The

Frederic Edwin Church, *The River of Light*, 1877

stream is metaphorically and spiritually *healing*, and it flows specifically from *Calvary's mountain*—rather than hill—to denote its elevated position.

In the second stanza, the variation on the main theme comes in the form of the speaker's testimony about the effect of the cross in her life. It is a conversion story in miniature, and the speaker steps forward to tell it as our representative and to express what we also have experienced.

The third stanza, which is cast as a prayer to Jesus, is a petition that he will implant the cross in the speaker's memory: that he will bring the scenes of the crucifixion to her mind and make the cross an overshadowing or governing presence within her daily walk of life.

The final stanza shifts from this petition to a statement. The speaker resolves and commits to live her entire earthly life oriented toward the cross. The refrain is likewise a statement of resolve that the cross will be the speaker's glory until her death.

The poetic power of the poem is amplified by the use of archetypes. These recurrent master images of literature and life are universal, and they tap very deep wellsprings of feeling. Examples in this poem are a *fountain*, a *stream*, a *mountain*, a *star* and its accompanying light, an overarching protective *shadow*, and the *golden strand* of the symbolic *river* that marks our transition to heaven at the moment we die. The poem is also a mosaic of famous Bible verses. There is no end to all that this seemingly simple poem packs into its mere four stanzas and refrain.

After assimilating the poem's thoughts and feelings about living near the cross, as well as the resolve that it offers in its refrain, we can profitably codify our own feelings on the subject and formulate our own statement of resolve based on it. ■

Much of the imagery of this hymnic poem comes from the book of Revelation, and it also contains a consistent eschatological thread that evokes pictures of the heavenly destination of those who allow themselves to be kept near the cross of Jesus. Its opening stanza draws upon Revelation 22:1–2:

> Then the angel showed me the river of the water of life, bright as crystal, flowing from the throne of God and of the Lamb . . . ; also, on either side of the river, the tree of life with its twelve kinds of fruit. . . . The leaves of the tree were for the healing of the nations.

The Old Rugged Cross

GEORGE BENNARD (1873–1958)

On a hill far away stood an old rugged cross,
the emblem of suffering and shame;
and I love that old cross where the dearest and best
for a world of lost sinners was slain.

O that old rugged cross, so despised by the world,
has a wondrous attraction for me;
for the dear Lamb of God left his glory above
to bear it to dark Calvary.

In that old rugged cross, stained with blood so divine,
a wondrous beauty I see,
for 'twas on that old cross Jesus suffered and died,
to pardon and sanctify me.

To that old rugged cross I will ever be true,
its shame and reproach gladly bear;
then he'll call me some day to my home far away,
where his glory forever I'll share.

Refrain
So I'll cherish the old rugged cross,
till my trophies at last I lay down;
I will cling to the old rugged cross,
and exchange it some day for a crown. ■

WE NEED TO BEGIN BY noting the extreme popularity of this hymn. It is regularly referred to as the most popular hymn of the twentieth century. It has been sung and recorded by so many celebrity singers that it ranks as a cultural icon.

The story of the hymn's origin is almost as famous as the hymn. The author was a Methodist evangelist whose home base was Albion, Michigan. The song belongs to a small circle of hymns whose music came before its words were composed to match the tune. The only words that initially came to the author were those of the opening line—words that he carried in his mind for days. The remainder came to him after he returned from an evangelistic crusade in New York where disruptive teenagers had ridiculed him. Returning to Michigan, he reflected on the meaning that the cross held in his life. According to Bennard, "The flood gates were loosed," and he quickly finished the hymn.

We need to dispel two objections that have unfairly stigmatized this hymn in some circles. First, the poem does not venerate a physical object but instead exalts the death that Jesus suffered on the cross. It does what Isaac Watts's parallel hymn does: it "surveys," or ponders, the cross in its

Crucifixion, early 1400s

various dimensions. The resolve, which the refrain expresses, to *cling to the cross* has the same meaning as other writers' commitment to stay *beneath the cross* and *near the cross*.

Second, far from sentimentalizing the cross, this hymn handles it in a thoroughly realistic manner. The cross is *rugged* or roughly hewn. It is not a polished crucifix in a church but *the emblem of suffering and shame*. It is *despised by the world* and *stained with blood*. To claim allegiance to it brings *shame and reproach* into one's life. As for the adjective *old*, in this context it is a term of definition. The cross on which Jesus died is literally old—two thousand years old. The word also denotes the cross's reliability and perpetual availability, as in the phrase *old standby*.

The first stanza of the hymn adheres to the centuries-old convention of composing the scene that the remainder of the poem will present for contemplation and analysis. Composing the scene activates our imagination, while the analysis that follows it awakens our understanding—in this case, our understanding of Jesus' sacrificial death on the cross. The poem's middle two stanzas follow a rhetorical pattern of repetition in which their first two lines assert that the cross, with all its external horror, holds an *attraction* and *beauty* for the speaker and for us, and their next two lines give the reason for this attraction, which is signaled each time by the word *for*.

The final stanza takes the familiar eschatological turn found in many hymns, as the speaker asserts his undying allegiance to the cross and his certainty that it will be the basis of his eventual entry into heaven. The chorus follows this same contour of allegiance to the cross as the gate to immortal life in heaven, along with adding the idea of renouncing all claims of human merit or achievement, which are summed up by the word *trophies*.

This poem prompts us to consider two things about the cross and the salvation that was accomplished on it: (1) the costliness of the cross for both Jesus and his followers and (2) the centrality that the cross needs to claim in our lives. ■

This hymnic poem follows the same pattern that the apostle Paul lays before us in Galatians 6:14: ". . . far be it from me to boast except in the cross of our Lord Jesus Christ, by which the world has been crucified to me, and I to the world."

AT THE OPEN TOMB

RESURRECTION

The poems in the previous units were notable for their variety of subject matter and theological viewpoint. Their authors' approach was partly analytic and reflective, though of course poetry is always the voice of emotion as well.

The poems in this resurrection unit are not analytic in the way that the poems on the crucifixion and atonement are. The primary business of poetry of the resurrection is to celebrate a victory. We might predict that this more single-minded purpose would become monotonous, but the reverse is the case. We are delighted at every turn of the poets' ingenuity as they express the joy of the resurrection and awaken it in their readers. Electricity breathes through their words. ■

Christ the Lord Is Risen Today

Charles Wesley (1707–1788)

Christ the Lord is risen today,
Sons of men and angels say.
Raise your joys and triumphs high;
Sing, ye heavens, and earth reply.

Vain the stone, the watch, the seal;
Christ has burst the gates of hell.
Death in vain forbids him rise;
Christ has opened paradise.

Lives again our glorious King;
Where, O death, is now thy sting?
Once he died, our souls to save;
Where thy victory, O grave?

Soar we now where Christ has led,
Following our exalted head.
Made like him, like him we rise;
Ours the cross, the grave, the skies. ■

It is appropriate to begin this unit on the resurrection of Jesus with the best-known Protestant Easter hymn. Its opening line, *Christ the Lord is risen today*, is a twofold announcement. *Today* signifies both the event of Christ's resurrection and also the occasion of Easter as it has been celebrated throughout history. Once its opening line has established the event and the occasion, the rest of the poem elaborates on its unifying declaration.

The primary business of the poem is a celebration and outpouring of emotion, and lines 2 through 4 of its opening stanza unleash the first volley. These lines issue four commands (*say*, *raise*, *sing*, *reply*) through a technique known as *apostrophe*—a direct address to beings who are absent but are treated as though they are present and capable of hearing and responding. Apostrophe is a standard way of expressing strong feeling.

The second stanza situates us at the open tomb. Here the poet employs the technique of a victory taunt on a battlefield. The phrase *in vain* declares that the obstacles to Christ's everlasting life have been defeated. The best efforts that his enemies could muster were powerless to keep him in the grave.

The battle and triumph motifs carry forward into the third stanza. The two pairs of lines in this stanza follow the same rhetorical pattern as each other, in which the first line names an action that Jesus performed and the second line is a taunting

Edvard Munch, *The Sun*, 1911

rhetorical question addressed to the personified entities of *death* and the *grave* respectively.

The final stanza marks a distinct shift from the preceding ones, but the same spirit of triumph and celebration carries into it. This stanza shifts from a focus on what Jesus did to what we do. John Wesley chose the motif of viewing the risen Christ as the *exalted head* or victor who leads his followers along the same path of *cross*, *grave*, and *skies* (eternal life in heaven) that he himself first trod.

The distinguishing trait of this poem, and the reason for its grip on us, is the spirit of exuberance that it expresses and awakens. One of the techniques by which the poem achieves this is its rhetorical pattern of pairs (e.g., *joys and triumphs*) and triplets (e.g., *the stone, the watch, the seal*) of items, which leads us to feel that stating only one of these things would be totally inadequate for fully expressing the situation. To this should be added the exuberant vocabulary that sweeps us into its orbit: *raise*, *high*, *burst*, *soar*, *exalted*, *rise*.

The devotional purpose of this poem is to awaken a range of appropriate feelings regarding Christ's resurrection. ■

The taunt that the apostle Paul addresses to death and the grave in 1 Corinthians 15:55 is directly referenced in the third stanza of "Christ the Lord Is Risen Today" and can be viewed as the subtext of the entire poem: "O death, where is thy sting? O grave, where is thy victory?" (KJV).

Boëtius Adamsz Bolswert, *An Angel Appears before the Three Marys at the Tomb*, 1590–1622

The Day of Resurrection!

John of Damascus (ca. 675–754)
Translated by John Mason Neale (1818–1866)

The day of resurrection!
Earth, tell it out abroad,
The Passover of gladness,
The Passover of God.
From death to life eternal,
From earth unto the sky,
Our Christ hath brought us over
With hymns of victory.

Our hearts be pure from evil,
That we may see aright
The Lord in rays eternal
Of resurrection light;
And, listening to his accents,
May hear, so calm and plain,
His own "All hail!" and hearing,
May raise the victor strain.

Now let the heavens be joyful,
Let earth her song begin;
Let the round world keep triumph,
And all that is therein;
Invisible and visible,
Their notes let all things blend,
For Christ the Lord hath risen,
Our joy that hath no end. ■

THIS POEM IS LOOSELY ORGANIZED, and once we realize this, we can be at ease as we navigate it. Its central thrust is to command people and cosmic entities to be joyful because Christ has risen from the dead. Issuing commands to rejoice is a standard feature of the praise psalms of the Old Testament, which doubtless served as a model for the poet. The effect of incessant commands to rejoice is to awaken and express the very joy they command. Each stanza presents its own variation on this central motif.

Stanza 1 begins by introducing the subject of the poem: *the day of resurrection*. The second line issues a command to the earth to proclaim this day, followed by two lines that present exalted epithets, or titles, for that day. Both epithets draw upon the Old Testament Passover, when the angel of death passed over the houses of the Israelites. This image of release from death leads directly to the brief narrative of deliverance that the rest of the opening stanza presents, in which Christ is said to have brought us over from death to life and from this world to the next.

In the second stanza, it is not the earth but we ourselves who are commanded to *be pure from evil*. Following this command, the rest of stanza 2 names two outcomes of our obedience: we will *see* the Lord in *resurrection light*, and we will *hear* Christ's consoling greeting *"All hail!"* which is how he greeted the women at the empty tomb (Matt. 28:9 KJV).

In the third stanza, the heavens and earth are variously commanded to *be joyful*, *begin* their *song*, *keep triumph*, and *their notes blend*. The reason for these commands, which is stated in the last two lines and signaled with the causal word *for*, sums up the twofold subject of the entire poem: *Christ the Lord hath risen* (the event that generates the commands), resulting in *our joy that hath no end*.

Within the simple framework of commands, the poem encompasses more than we might think. Its objects of address are nothing less than the heavens, the earth (including *all that is therein*, *invisible and visible*), and the company of the redeemed. Each stanza adds more and more to an ongoing to-do list, and the reasons the poem names for joy, as well as the ways its says to express it, keep multiplying.

The application of this poem is to do what it commands: be joyful because the day of resurrection has come. ■

The resurrection is the fulfillment of Old Testament premonitions, as we see when we place a christological overlay on Old Testament passages that command God's people to rejoice. Isaiah 44:23 is an example: "Sing, O heavens, for the Lord has done it; shout, O depths of the earth; break forth into singing, O mountains."

Plaque with the Holy Women at the Sepulchre, ca. 1140–60

Most Glorious Lord of Life

EDMUND SPENSER (1552–1599)

Most glorious Lord of life, that on this day
Didst make thy triumph over death and sin,
And having harrowed hell didst bring away
Captivity thence captive, us to win:
This joyous day, dear Lord, with joy begin,
And grant that we for whom thou didst die,
Being with thy dear blood clean washed from sin,
May live forever in felicity.
And that thy love we weighing worthily,
May likewise love thee for the same again,
And for thy sake, that all like dear didst buy,
With love may one another entertain.
So let us love, dear love, like as we ought,
Love is the lesson which the Lord us taught. ■

COMPOSED BY A TOWERING FIGURE of English literature, this sonnet is one of the most unusual Easter poems ever written. It is sonnet 68 in what was known in the sixteenth century as a *sonnet sequence* or *sonnet cycle*—a collection of romantic love sonnets on the theme of a single, usually fictional, courtship. Spenser was a widower when he wrote this sonnet cycle about his real-life courtship of his second wife. Putting all this together, we can see that "Most Glorious Lord of Life" is an Easter love sonnet addressed to the poet's fiancée.

The sonnet's first twelve lines are a prayer addressed to the risen Lord. When the poet speaks in the opening line of *this day*, he means Easter, the day of resurrection. In the last two lines, he turns to his beloved and issues a command to both her and himself that grows out of that prayer. In keeping with the conventions of the English sonnet form, these last two self-contained lines are a rhyming couplet that sums up what has preceded it.

It is also characteristic of the sonnet form that the first twelve lines fall into a pattern of three four-line units of thought called *quatrains*. This helps us to fine-tune our understanding of the poem's organization. Lines 1 through 4 are not a complete sentence but instead an opening

Copy after David Teniers II, *Wedding Feast*, late 17th century

invocation to Christ that is built around references to his death and resurrection. Lines 5 through 12 follow this invocation with a threefold petition that those who have been *washed from sin* will (1) *live forever in felicity*, (2) respond to Christ's love by loving him in turn, and (3) love their fellow believers. The concluding exhortation encompasses the two main themes of the sonnet: Christ's love, as shown through his death and resurrection, and the love that Christians should display as they emulate their Lord.

The biographical foundation of the poem does not affect its universality. Its first twelve lines use the second-person plural pronoun (*we*, *us*), the way many of the psalms do. The sentiments that they express thus expand beyond the speaker and his fiancée to encompass all Christians. This is true of even the concluding couplet, which Christians can use to exhort one another and themselves.

The poem is a mosaic of evocative New Testament allusions. To cite just one example, the reference in lines 3 and 4 to Christ's descent into death, from which he then brought back captives, echoes the picture that Ephesians 4:8–10 paints of Christ as the one who "descended into the lower regions, the earth" and then "ascended [leading] a host of captives." Even when Spenser does not allude to specific passages, the language and sentiments of his poem remind us continually of the New Testament.

The poem deserves to be pondered slowly line by line, and when we do this, we can internalize everything that is in it. Additionally, the particular slant that it offers on the resurrection is the emphasis it places on the mutual love between Christ and believers. ■

Spenser's sonnet is a miniature discourse on love—Christ's love for his followers and their love for Christ and one another. Christ's words to his disciples during his Upper Room Discourse sound the same notes: "This is my commandment, that you love one another as I have loved you" (John 15:12).

Jean-Baptiste Patas, *Three Marys at the Empty Tomb*, 1789–1807

The Strife Is O'er, the Battle Done

Author Unknown (seventeenth century)
Translated by Francis Pott (1832–1909)

The strife is o'er, the battle done;
The victory of life is won;
The song of triumph has begun.

The powers of death have done their worst,
But Christ their legions hath dispersed:
Let shouts of holy joy outburst.

The three sad days have quickly sped;
He rises glorious from the dead:
All glory to our risen head!

He closed the yawning gates of hell;
The bars from heaven's high portals fell:
Let hymns of praise his triumphs tell.

Lord, by the stripes which wounded thee,
From death's dread sting thy servants free,
That we may live and sing to thee. ■

This hymnic poem celebrates Christ's victory over death and hell, which has freed all who trust in him. The apostle Paul, as he writes to the Colossians, lays the groundwork for the poem's theme: "[Christ] disarmed the rulers and authorities and put them to open shame, by triumphing over them in [the cross]" (2:15).

The controlling idea for this entire poem is announced by its opening line: Christ has won the victory in the greatest battle ever waged. Composed in Latin during the seventeenth century and later translated by an Anglican clergyman, this poem places itself in a tradition dating back to the Middle Ages that is known by the Latin phrase *Christus Victor* (Christ the Victor). The imagery of conflict and victory characterizes every stanza of this poem. To find the answer to what Christ triumphed *over,* we need to allow the poem itself to explain what the author had in mind.

Turning to the poem, we can immediately see the simplicity of its design. The individual stanzas have only three lines, and those three lines share a single rhyming sound. To make it even easier to progress through the poem, the poet constructed each stanza on a principle of symmetry that unifies them all. The first two lines of each stanza assert something about the resurrection, and the third line responds joyfully. As these opening pairs of lines unfold, they give us a progressive explanation of the ways in which Christ triumphed through his resurrection. As we ponder each individual stanza's assertions, the poem becomes much more complex than its surface simplicity originally leads us to think.

We can trace the poem's variations on its main theme as follows. Its opening stanza introduces the motifs of conflict and triumph in general terms, and the phrase *victory of life* alerts us to the fact that this is an Easter poem. Carrying this motif forward into the next stanza, the poem identifies *the powers of death* as the enemy that has been vanquished, and when these powers are called *legions*, we are not only led to picture vast hosts of demonic forces but also reminded of the time when Jesus cast out a demon who called himself *Legion* (Mark 5:9; Luke 8:30). Christ has triumphed over Satan and his hosts.

The middle stanza, by mentioning *three sad days* and rising *from the dead*, takes us to the empty tomb on the morning of the resurrection. The fourth stanza transports us from the enclosed garden of the tomb to the cosmic realms of hell, whose *yawning gates* have been *closed*, and heaven, whose *bars* have been torn open to allow entry. In the final stanza, the poet turns in prayer to his *Lord* and clinches the Easter theme by declaring that we have been freed *from death's dread sting*.

We will feel this poem's devotional effect as we ponder Jesus' resurrection as a victory over death and Satan and allow ourselves to follow its prompts to rejoice. ■

Guglielmus Paludanus, *The Resurrection*, 1565–1665

Easter

GEORGE HERBERT (1593–1633)

I got me flowers to straw thy way;
I got me boughs off many a tree;
But thou wast up by break of day
And broughtest thy sweets along with thee.

The sun arising in the east,
Though he give light, and the East perfume,
If they should offer to contest
With thy arising, they presume.

Can there be any day but this,
Though many suns to shine endeavor?
We count three hundred, but we miss:
There is but one, and that one ever. ■

THE POEM "EASTER" MAY SEEM obscure on the surface, but any mystery is easily clarified if we follow the lead of an experienced tour guide. From time immemorial, poets who have written in praise of a person or event have used a technique of comparison; they set their subject alongside an acknowledged standard of excellence, such as the beauty of nature, and then declare their subject to be superior to that standard. That is what George Herbert does in this poem. In each stanza he compares the resurrection of Jesus to something that is obviously excellent, then asserts that the resurrection is even better. The central theme of this Easter poem is therefore the surpassing greatness of Christ's resurrection. The resurrection not only surpasses even the best alternative but in fact cancels it.

Although the technique of comparison is familiar, Herbert was a poet who cultivated innovative ways of expressing truth. For example, he begins the poem in an expected way by composing the scene, but he does so with a surprise twist. We expect an Easter poem to take our imaginations to the garden of the empty tomb. Instead, Herbert pictures himself rising early on Easter morning and walking from his parsonage into the surrounding countryside to gather *flowers* and *boughs* for Easter. This was a ritual that was practiced in the rural England of Herbert's day, as people celebrated annual events such as Christmas and May Day by bringing greenery into their villages or homes. The opening two lines of this poem amplify this tradition by alluding to Christ's triumphal entry on Palm Sunday as well. But the speaker's determination to "do things right" on Easter morning is gently rebuked. Jesus is pictured as having already brought his own *sweets*, or festive decorations. In this poetic way, Herbert claims that Jesus' resurrection is greater than any commemoration of it that we can orchestrate.

The poem's next two stanzas enact a similar process of comparison by declaring Jesus' resurrection to be so superior that it renders other things inferior and even superfluous. In stanza 2, the sun that is rising in the East, along with perfumes that have been imported from Asia, are presumptuous if they think they can compete for glory with the resurrection of Jesus. Similarly, no number of sunrises can match the splendor of Easter day, and even though we calculate 365 days in a year (which the poem rounds off to "three hundred"), Easter day is so important as to completely supplant all the other days. The poem thus uses hyperbole to assert the supreme value of Easter day and of Christ's resurrection from the dead.

As we leave Herbert's innovative poem, we can affirm with it that Christ's resurrection is of surpassing value in our lives. ■

Herbert's theme of the surpassing greatness of Christ's resurrection finds a parallel in Ephesians 1:18–20, in which the apostle Paul prays

> that you may know . . . what are the riches of his glorious inheritance in the saints, and what is the immeasurable greatness of his power toward us who believe, according to the working of his great might that he worked in Christ when he raised him from the dead.

Vincent van Gogh, *Wheat Field with Reaper and Sun*, 1889

Thine Is the Glory

Edmond L. Budry (1854–1932)
Translated by Richard B. Hoyle (1875–1939)

Thine is the glory, risen, conquering Son;
Endless is the vict'ry thou o'er death hast won.
Angels in bright raiment rolled the stone away,
Kept the folded grave-clothes where thy body lay.

Lo! Jesus meets us, risen from the tomb;
Lovingly he greets us, scatters fear and gloom;
Let his church with gladness hymns of triumph sing,
For her Lord now liveth; death has lost its sting.

No more we doubt thee, glorious prince of life!
Life is nought without thee; aid us in our strife;
Make us more than conquerors through thy deathless love;
Bring us safe through Jordan to thy home above. ■

The entire progression of this triumphant Easter poem is foreshadowed in its opening line. This line ascribes glory to Christ and gives him the evocative epithet *risen, conquering Son*. The three governing motifs of all the poem's stanzas are laid out in this single line.

One of these motifs, which is suggested by the adjective *risen*, is an imagining of the circumstances that surround the resurrection itself. Thus in the opening stanza we look into the empty tomb with our own eyes and see the *folded grave-clothes*. In the middle stanza, we join the women at the tomb as they are met and greeted by Jesus on the first Easter morning. The third stanza's claim that *no more we doubt thee* places us at Jesus' post-resurrection appearance to doubting Thomas. When Jesus commands us, "Do not disbelieve, but believe," we reply with Thomas, "My Lord and my God" (John 20:27–28). We expect an Easter poem to rehearse the events of the resurrection, and this poem does so in every stanza.

A. A. Ivanov, *Christ's Appearance to Mary Magdalene after the Resurrection*, 1835

In addition to introducing the motif of Jesus as *risen*, the opening line calls him a *conquering Son*. As we progress through the poem, we find that every stanza treats the resurrection as a battle victory. Line 2 speaks of the *vict'ry* that Christ won over death. The next stanza commands the church to sing *hymns of triumph*. In the last stanza, Jesus is called the *glorious prince of life*, and his followers ask for *aid* in their *strife* and to be made *more than conquerors*. The motif of battle that ends in victory is thus a second controlling theme in this song of triumph.

The poem's third controlling motif is the spirit of exuberance that breathes through every line of the poem. The opening line ascribes *glory* to the *risen* and *conquering Son*. The second stanza enjoins the church to *sing* with *gladness*. In the last stanza, we hope to become *more than conquerors*. All the assertions in the poem are fired by a spirit of celebration through this vocabulary of exultation. Their power is intensified when the poem is sung as a hymn to the rousing music of George Frideric Handel's chorus from *Judas Maccabaeus* "See, the Conqu'ring Hero Comes!"

Some features of the hymn's poetic form further explain why it is so explosive. Its lines are longer and fuller than is usual: the first in each stanza consists of ten syllables, and the three that follow have eleven syllables each. This feature lends the quality of a victory march to the poem. Its couplet rhyme scheme, consisting of consecutive pairs of lines that rhyme with each other, gives it further energy.

The right way to absorb the devotional impact of this poem is to give ourselves to its mood of triumph. ■

This hymnic poem owes its exuberant tone to Romans 8:31–39. Here is a brief selection from that passage: "If God is for us, who can be against us? . . . Christ Jesus is the one who died—more than that, who was raised. . . . We are more than conquerors through him who loved us" (vv. 31, 34, 37).

Erasmus Quellinus II, *Saint Thomas Touching Christ's Wounds*, 1644

Easter Hymn

Henry Vaughan (1621–1695)

Death and darkness, get you packing,
Nothing now to man is lacking,
All your triumphs now are ended,
And what Adam marred is mended.
Graves are beds now for the weary,
Death a nap, to wake more merry;
Youth now, full of pious duty,
Seeks in thee for perfect beauty;
The weak and aged tired with length
Of days, from thee look for new strength;
And infants with thy pangs contest
As pleasant, as if with the breast.
Then, unto him who thus hath thrown
Even to contempt thy kingdom down,
And by his blood did us advance
Unto his own inheritance,
To him be glory, power, praise,
From this, unto the last of days. ■

THE MAJORITY OF EASTER POEMS and hymns are written in what literary scholars call the *high style*: they feature dignified language, exalted sentiment, stately epithets (titles for persons or things), and conventional poetic and rhetorical devices such as metaphors and parallel clauses. Henry Vaughan's poem positions itself in an alternate style that can be called *colloquial* or *conversational,* and we can relish it as a change from the poems that have preceded it in this anthology. When Vaughan titled this poem a *hymn,* he did not mean that he intended for it to be sung in church. In standard poetic terminology, a *hymn* can be simply a poem on a religious subject.

The overall genre of the poem fits its informal tone. The hymn is a taunt or putdown of death, which is personified (treated as a person) and treated with scorn. The opening line strikes this note with its command *get you packing*. In our own common parlance, that is approximately the same as *get lost* or *scram*—something we might say to a squirrel on our doorstep. With the style of the poem thus established right at the outset, the door is open for us to enjoy the ingenious ways in which the poet celebrates his superiority over death.

Vaughan wrote in the same style as his mentor John Donne, which means that he strove to express truth in unconventional ways. As a result, we need to take just a little more time than usual to figure out what his given metaphors and other expressions mean. We can do this more readily if we realize how Vaughan supports his claim that death is a puny adversary: he gives specific examples of how various age groups may embrace death as something positive and desirable because it draws them to an afterlife of bliss.

The putdown of death constitutes the first two-thirds of Vaughan's poem. As the speaker unloads his volley of scorn, we gradually begin to wonder how he dares to do so. The poem shifts gears and gives us the answer in its last third, as the speaker moves from taunting death to describing the basis for his (and our) confidence. The style becomes more formal as the poet outlines how the atonement provided by Jesus' blood has defeated death on behalf of all who believe. The assurance that we feel as we read these six lines is bolstered by the form in which they are cast: a benediction in the mode of those in the Bible.

This poem's devotional application is for us to take to heart that we need not fear death, recognizing that we have a strong theological foundation for this confidence. ■

The last six lines of "Easter Hymn" are a collation of famous New Testament benedictions. One of them is from Jude: "Now to him who is able to . . . present you blameless before the presence of his glory with great joy, to the only God, our Savior, through Jesus Christ our Lord, be glory, majesty, dominion, and authority, before all time and now and forever. Amen" (vv. 24–25).

He Qi, *Resurrection*, no date

Come, Ye Faithful, Raise the Strain

John of Damascus (ca. 675–754)
Translated by John Mason Neale (1818–1866)

Come, ye faithful, raise the strain
Of triumphant gladness;
God hath brought his Israel
Into joy from sadness;
Loosed from Pharaoh's bitter yoke
Jacob's sons and daughters;
Led them with unmoistened foot
Through the Red Sea waters.

'Tis the spring of souls today;
Christ hath burst his prison,
And from three days' sleep in death
As a sun hath risen;
All the winter of our sins,
Long and dark, is flying
From his light, to whom we give
Laud and praise undying.

Now the queen of seasons, bright
With the day of splendor,
With the royal feast of feasts,
Comes its joy to render;
Comes to glad Jerusalem,
Who with true affection
Welcomes in unwearied strains
Jesus' resurrection.

Neither might the gates of death,
Nor the tomb's dark portal,
Nor the watchers, nor the seal
Hold thee as a mortal:
But today amidst the twelve
Thou didst stand, bestowing
That thy peace, which evermore
Passeth human knowing. ■

THE PREVIOUS ENTRY REPRESENTED A STYLISTIC change from the preceding poems in this unit, and this poem represents a change at the level of content. Here too we can relish the innovation that is presented to us. As one example, the poem's first and third stanzas do a great deal more with Old Testament foreshadowing than we expect in an Easter poem. Yet there is enough that is familiar to allay any doubt that this indeed is a resurrection hymn.

Although the poem's first two lines are exactly what we would expect to sing at an Easter service, the rest of the opening stanza immerses us in Israel's exodus from Egypt and crossing of the Red Sea. What is this doing in an Easter poem? The poet is speaking metaphorically. The Israelites' deliverance from bondage is *like* the deliverance from death that Jesus has secured for us through his resurrection. Because the original Passover involved sprinkling blood on a doorpost, we naturally connect it with the events of Good Friday, and we recall that on the night of the last plague, God's people were protected from the angel of death. With this

Lidia Kozenitzky, *KriatYamSoof*, 2009

as the basis for our comparison, we can ponder the connections that the opening stanza makes between Passover and Easter.

The second stanza treads familiar resurrection territory, but here too the author gives us more than a conventional treatment of his subject. In particular, he effectively uses nature imagery—*spring*, *sun*, *winter*, *dark*, and *light*—as symbols of spiritual and emotional realities.

The third stanza returns us to Old Testament prefigurings of Easter. We are imaginatively placed not in the garden of the tomb but in the adjoining city of Jerusalem, where Jesus appeared after his resurrection. *The royal feast of feasts* is the Passover, which Jesus now fulfills. *Glad Jerusalem* is a personification that is used to represent Old Testament believers and, by extension, the community of believers in Christ. Interwoven with these images is a winsome thread of the vocabulary of joy, featuring such words as *bright*, *splendor*, *joy*, *glad*, *true affection*, and *unwearied*. The stanza is an exuberant uplift.

The final stanza is solidly anchored in the first Easter through its references to *the watchers*, *the seal*, and Jesus' standing *amidst the twelve* disciples. The poem thus shuttles back and forth between the unexpected and expected. The exuberant tone of the poem joins these elements into a coherent whole.

When we read this poem devotionally, it can lead us both to ponder how Easter relates to the Old Testament and to celebrate Easter with appropriate joy. ■

"Come, Ye Faithful, Raise the Strain" celebrates Jesus' resurrection as bringing full meaning to what was latent in ages past. Second Timothy 1:10 speaks in similar terms about "the appearing of our Savior Christ Jesus, who abolished death and brought life and immortality to light through the gospel."

Jan Luyken, *The Passover*, no date

RAISED WITH CHRIST

LIFE EVERLASTING

Earlier parts of this anthology focused on *redemption accomplished* and *redemption applied*. The framework of accomplishment and application can be applied to the poetry of the resurrection as well.

The preceding unit celebrated what happened at the empty tomb. But resurrection did not end on the first Easter. Its effects are applied to every believer, preeminently in the immortality of their souls in the life to come. That is what the poems in this unit explore. The reflective element that gave way to celebration now returns, as the poets in this section analyze the effects that Jesus' resurrection has in believers' lives.

The last two entries in this unit combine references to the cross and to the resurrection, which lends a final synthesis to this anthology. ■

Jesus Lives, and So Shall I

Christian F. Gellert (1715–1769)
Translated by John Dunmore Lang (1799–1878)

Jesus lives, and so shall I.
Death! thy sting is gone forever!
He who deigned for me to die,
Lives, the bands of death to sever.
He shall raise me from the dust:
Jesus is my hope and trust.

Jesus lives, and reigns supreme,
And, his kingdom still remaining,
I shall also be with him,
Ever living, ever reigning.
God has promised: be it must:
Jesus is my hope and trust.

Jesus lives, and by his grace,
Victory o'er my passions giving,
I will cleanse my heart and ways,
Ever to his glory living.
Me he raises from the dust.
Jesus is my hope and trust.

Jesus lives, I know full well
Naught from him my heart can sever,
Life nor death nor powers of hell,
Joy nor grief, hence forth forever.
None of all his saints is lost;
Jesus is my hope and trust.

Jesus lives, and death is now
But my entrance into glory.
Courage, then, my soul, for thou
Hast a crown of life before thee;
Thou shalt find thy hopes were just;
Jesus is the Christian's trust. ■

POEMS IN THE PREVIOUS UNIT celebrated Jesus' triumph over death. Poems in this unit turn our attention to the effects of his resurrection in the life of a believer. The opening line of this poem sounds the keynote of this unit when it links our own immortality to the resurrection of Jesus. The poem's main structural element is an ever-expanding list of the blessings and assurances that flow from Jesus' resurrection, with emphasis on the immortality of a believer's soul.

Every stanza of the poem begins with a declaration that *Jesus lives*. Each one concludes with a line that asserts that *Jesus is my hope and trust*, though the last stanza's line slightly alters this. Between these two ideas, the meditation unfolds. Stanza by stanza, we are led to ponder a sequence of variations on the main theme of what Jesus' resurrection means in a believer's life. If we are alert, we can see that a second resurrection theme of *ongoing* life is subtly present throughout the poem as well.

The opening stanza features a taunt addressed directly to death. The analysis that follows leads us to see that Jesus' ability to *sever* the shackles or *bands of death*, even after our physical bodies lie in the *dust*, is due to the fact that he *lives* (the resurrection theme). Everything is concrete in this stanza, and its images make its assertions come alive in our imagination.

The second stanza repeats the first stanza's idea that because Jesus is *ever living*, he is able to perform his divine acts without end. The specific sphere of divine action in this stanza is Jesus' reign over a kingdom that is *still remaining* (eternal), in which believers will *ever* live and reign with him.

The third stanza flows logically from the second stanza's idea that believers are part of the ongoing kingdom of Christ. As a citizen of that kingdom, the speaker in the poem resolves to undertake what the Puritans called a *holy reformation* of his life, thereby *ever living* to Christ's glory.

Jan Luyken, *Heaven's Gate*, 1708–10

The fourth stanza draws upon Romans 8 and its list of things that cannot separate us from God; keeping with its resurrection theme, it concludes that these things will remain unable to sever us from God *forever*.

The final stanza takes the eschatological turn that is a convention of hymns, moving to consider the afterlife of believers in *glory*. On a rhetorical level, the speaker replaces the poem's declarative mode with one of self-address as he speaks to his own soul. And just as the repeated concluding line of each stanza (*Jesus is my hope and trust*) threatens to become monotonous, the poet breaks from the formula to say, more comprehensively, *Jesus is the* Christian's *trust*.

Our devotional takeaway here is twofold: following the lead of the poem, we can undertake our own meditation on the implications that Jesus' resurrection has for our eternal wellbeing, and we can renew our assurance of these resurrection truths. ■

This hymn links the believer's resurrection at the last day with Christ's resurrection. Jesus' words in John 11:25–26 do the same: "I am the resurrection and the life. Whoever believes in me, though he die, yet shall he live, and everyone who lives and believes in me shall never die."

Charles Mottram after John Martin, *The Plains of Heaven*, 1857

Death, Be Not Proud

John Donne (1572–1631)

Death, be not proud, though some have called thee
Mighty and dreadful, for thou art not so;
For those whom thou thinkest thou dost overthrow
Die not, poor Death, nor yet canst thou kill me.
From rest and sleep, which but thy pictures be,
Much pleasure; then from thee much more must flow,
And soonest our best men with thee do go,
Rest of their bones, and soul's delivery.
Thou art slave to fate, chance, kings, and desperate men,
And dost with poison, war, and sickness dwell;
And poppy or charms can make us sleep as well
And better than thy stroke; why swellest thou then?
One short sleep past, we wake eternally,
And death shall be no more; Death, thou shalt die. ■

THROUGH THE AGES, THE MOST common view of death has led us to fear and dread it. The imagery through which this view is often expressed presents death as a powerful and fearsome enemy that is engaged in single combat with every living person. John Donne defiantly refutes this common view.

The result is the most famous poem on immortality in English literature. Its argument takes two approaches. One is to assert the immortality of the believer's soul. The other is to taunt death in a spirited putdown. Giving the poem a dramatic cast, the poem is directly addressed to a personified Death and takes the form of one half of an implied debate in which the speaker refutes Death's claims that it is powerful. The vigor that fires the speaker's rebuttal allows us to experience *what it feels like* to really believe in the resurrection of the body and eternal life.

Donne valued a style of poetry that is difficult and therefore requires our best efforts to unpack. We will be aided in our work if we know that this sonnet is organized by pairs of lines. Its first two lines are, in effect, a thesis statement. If we fast-forward to the last two lines, we see that they, like the opening two, are a taunt addressed directly to a personified Death.

Between these two bookends, the poem offers a sequence of two-line reasons why death should not be proud: death does not really kill people; it brings pleasure, just as sleep does; virtuous people actually desire death

and welcome it as a deliverance; death keeps very bad company and therefore has no reason to boast; and death is unnecessary, inasmuch as drugs can produce sleep better than it does. When the accumulation of all this evidence has piled up, the poet asks his climactic question: *Why swellest thou then?* (Why are you puffed up with pride?). The implied answer to this rhetorical question is that death has no reason whatsoever to be proud.

Evocative Bible verses and commonplaces converge in the poem: death is a sleep from which believers arise at the resurrection (Dan. 12:2), death is a welcome deliverance from earthly life and a means to reach heaven (Phil. 1:23), and in the age to come "death shall be no more" (Rev. 21:4).

This poem has the devotional impact of reinvigorating our conviction that in Christ we will live forever, and that it would therefore be a betrayal of our faith to fear death. ■

There is no doubt that Donne built his poem on the foundation of the famous taunt that Paul addresses to death in 1 Corinthians 15: "O death, where is your victory? O death, where is your sting? . . . Thanks be to God, who gives us the victory through our Lord Jesus Christ" (vv. 55, 57).

Paul Cézanne, *Still Life with Skull*, 1890–93

Our Resurrection at the Last Day

Selection from 1 Corinthians 15

But in fact Christ has been raised from the dead,
  the firstfruits of those who have fallen asleep.
For as by a man came death,
  by a man has come also the resurrection of the dead.
For as in Adam all die,
  so also in Christ shall all be made alive.
But each in his own order: Christ the firstfruits,
  then at his coming those who belong to Christ.

Then comes the end,
  when he delivers the kingdom to God the Father
  after destroying every rule and every authority and power.
For he must reign
  until he has put all his enemies under his feet.
The last enemy to be destroyed is death. . . .

Not all flesh is the same,
  but there is one kind for humans,
  another for animals,
  another for birds,
  and another for fish.
There are heavenly bodies and earthly bodies,
  but the glory of the heavenly is of one kind,
  and the glory of the earthly is of another.
There is one glory of the sun,
  and another glory of the moon,
  and another glory of the stars;
for star differs from star in glory.

So is it with the resurrection of the dead.
What is sown is perishable;
  what is raised is imperishable.

It is sown in dishonor;
  it is raised in glory.
It is sown in weakness;
  it is raised in power.
It is sown a natural body;
  it is raised a spiritual body.
If there is a natural body,
  there is also a spiritual body.

Thus it is written, "The first man Adam became a living being";
  the last Adam became a life-giving spirit.
But it is not the spiritual that is first but the natural,
  and then the spiritual.
The first man was from the earth,
  a man of dust;
the second man is from heaven.

As was the man of dust,
  so also are those who are of the dust,
and as is the man of heaven,
  so also are those who are of heaven.
Just as we have borne the image of the man of dust,
  we shall also bear the image of the man of heaven. . . .

Behold! I tell you a mystery.
We shall not all sleep, but we shall all be changed,
  in a moment,
  in the twinkling of an eye,
  at the last trumpet.
For the trumpet will sound,
  and the dead will be raised imperishable,
  and we shall be changed.
For this perishable body must put on the imperishable,
  and this mortal body must put on immortality. ■

What makes this passage so moving? It does not trivialize the passage at all to say that its poetic and rhetorical form are what enables it to achieve its effect. Its same content, if expressed in everyday expository prose, would inform our minds but not sweep us up into an ecstasy. The form or vehicle in which an utterance comes to us is not a mere decoration but is instead the heart and soul of the overall effect.

The first thing that draws our attention is the parallelism of the passage's phrases and clauses. There is a strong rhythm at work here, and we are aware of the rise and fall of the writer's language (its *cadence*), even when we read the passage silently. This cadence creates not only a sense of momentum but also a pattern of expectation. We have a saying about waiting for the other shoe to drop. That sense of anticipation governs this entire rhapsody on the resurrection body.

Imposed on this regular rhythm of phrases and clauses is the rhetorical device of repetition. Word patterns are part of this carefully orchestrated repetition, and so are what are called *formulas*. In the opening stanza, for example, we see the formula *for as . . . by* or *so also*. The principles of parallelism and balance feed into this construction as well.

But these are only the beginning of the rhetorical wonder of the passage. The entire passage is constructed on the principle of comparison and contrast. These contrasts fall into several categories and unify the passage. One of these is the contrast between the physical and the spiritual or the *earthly* and the *heavenly*. The contrasts in this category imply a qualitative difference—that the spiritual is better than the physical. Another type of contrast that is woven throughout the passage is a chronological one, in which the first manifestation of something is understood to be surpassed by the second or final one. For example, the *last Adam* (Christ) is greater than the *first Adam* and the *mortal body* is inferior to the immortal one.

What we have covered thus far falls into the category of *rhetoric,* meaning the conscious arrangement of material according to conventional patterns such as repetition and contrast. But the passage is also poetic, and as such its primary ingredients are imagery and metaphor. As we progress through the passage, we move in a sphere of sowing and reaping and *firstfruits* and *birds* and trumpets and *sun*, *moon*, and *stars*. The principle at work here is *analogy,* as the passage compares aspects of earthly and heavenly bodies to things that are like them.

Jan Lievens, *The Resurrection of Lazarus*, 1620–74

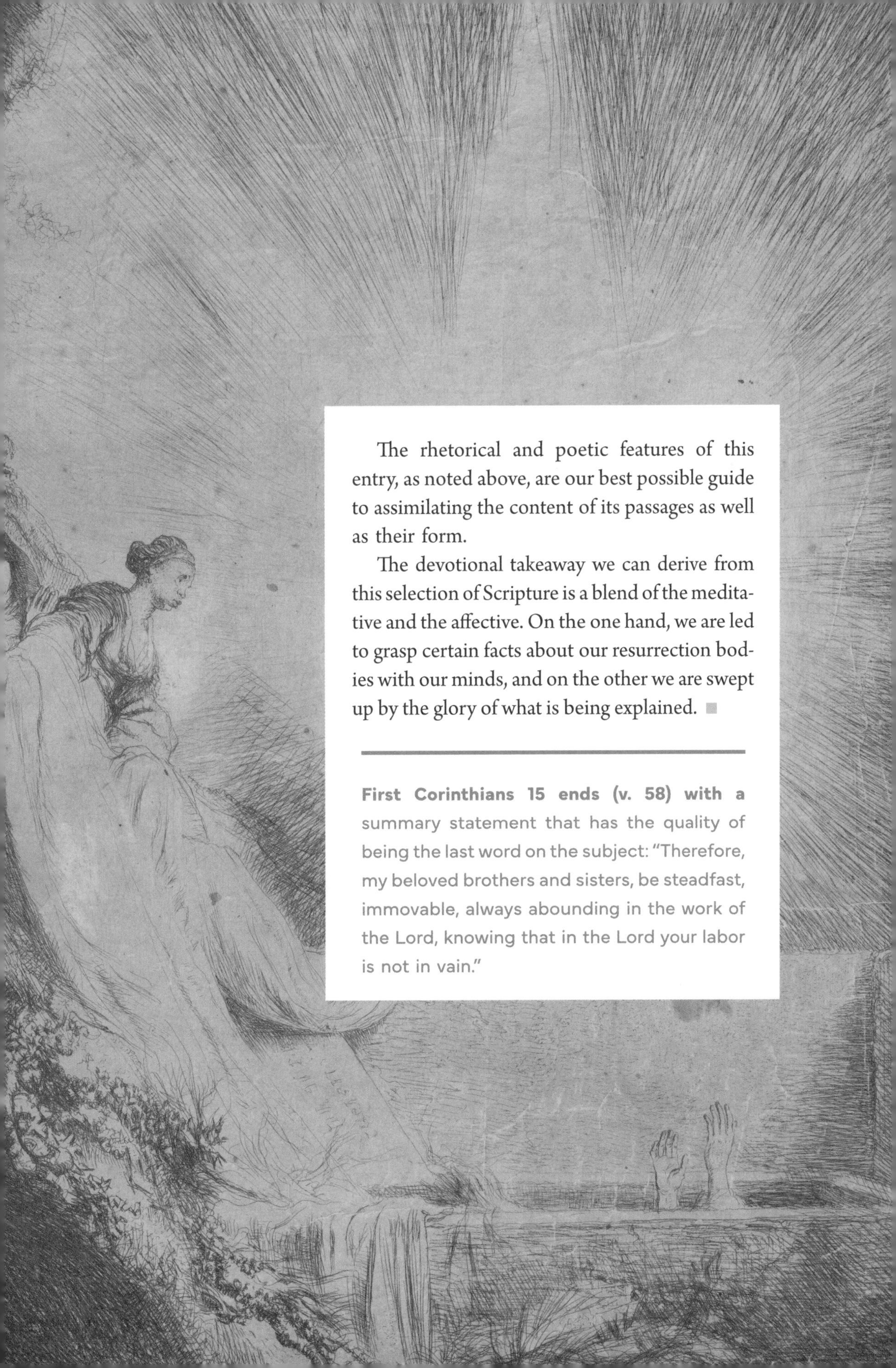

The rhetorical and poetic features of this entry, as noted above, are our best possible guide to assimilating the content of its passages as well as their form.

The devotional takeaway we can derive from this selection of Scripture is a blend of the meditative and the affective. On the one hand, we are led to grasp certain facts about our resurrection bodies with our minds, and on the other we are swept up by the glory of what is being explained. ■

First Corinthians 15 ends (v. 58) with a summary statement that has the quality of being the last word on the subject: "Therefore, my beloved brothers and sisters, be steadfast, immovable, always abounding in the work of the Lord, knowing that in the Lord your labor is not in vain."

The Believer's Riches in Christ

SELECTIONS FROM THE EPISTLES

Paul the Apostle

Blessed be the God and Father
   of our Lord Jesus Christ,
who has blessed us in Christ
   with every spiritual blessing in the heavenly places.
In him we have redemption through his blood,
   the forgiveness of our trespasses,
according to the riches of his grace.

The Father . . . has qualified you to share
   in the inheritance of the saints in light.
He has delivered us from the domain of darkness
   and transferred us to the kingdom of his beloved Son,
in whom we have redemption,
   the forgiveness of sins.

But when the goodness and loving kindness
   of God our Savior appeared,
he saved us, not because of works done by us in righteousness,
   but according to his own mercy,
by the washing of regeneration
   and renewal of the Holy Spirit,
whom he poured out on us richly
   through Jesus Christ our Savior,
so that being justified by his grace
   we might become heirs according to the hope of eternal life.

The Writer to the Hebrews

Now may the God of peace
who brought again from the dead our Lord Jesus,
the great shepherd of the sheep,
by the blood of the eternal covenant,
equip you with everything good
that you may do his will,
working in us that which is pleasing in his sight,
through Jesus Christ,
to whom be glory forever and ever. Amen.

Peter the Apostle

Blessed be the God and Father
of our Lord Jesus Christ!
According to his great mercy,
he caused us to be born again to a living hope
through the resurrection of Jesus Christ from the dead,
to an inheritance that is imperishable,
undefiled, and unfading,
kept in heaven for you,
who by God's power are being guarded through faith
for a salvation ready to be revealed in the last time.

His divine power has granted to us
all things that pertain to life and godliness,
through the knowledge of him who called us
to his own glory and excellence,
by which he has granted to us
his precious and very great promises,
so that through them you may become partakers
of the divine nature.
There will be richly provided for you
an entrance into the eternal kingdom
of our Lord and Savior Jesus Christ. ■

THE NEW TESTAMENT EPISTLES, THOUGH they are printed as prose in our English Bibles, are incipient poetry, fitting the category that literary scholars call *prose poetry* or *poetic prose*. All that is required to bring out their poetic quality is to arrange them in the verse form of all biblical poetry, parallelism. In addition to this rhythm of phrases and clauses, a lyric or emotional undertow repeatedly breaks above the surface of the epistles. Thus the selections printed above are right at home in this anthology of poetry.

Although poetic qualities appear at many points throughout the New Testament epistles, they are particularly concentrated in two subgenres of the epistolary form: the *thanksgiving* and the *benediction*. In the thanksgiving section, which usually appears early in an epistle, the author lists what he is thankful for as it relates to his intended audience. Often these thanksgivings rehearse the blessings that believers possess in Christ. The benediction often falls toward the end of the letter. In such a section, the writer blesses his readers directly.

Why do these poetic selections appear in an anthology of Holy Week poems? This selection shows that our primary riches in Christ—our perfected spiritual standing—come through Christ's death and resurrection. As we progress through the successive stanzas of this selection, we can be

alert to their references to the two primary subjects of this anthology: salvation through Christ's sacrifice and eternal life through his resurrection.

The primary structural element of this selection is the catalog or list. We can absorb its declarations as a spiritual inventory of what matters most in our lives. This inventory has the quality of a *charter*—a list of what members of a group possess by virtue of being its members. Its style and vocabulary are exalted. The parallelism of its clauses lends it not only beauty of expression but also a formality and eloquence befitting such a grand subject. Its sentences are long, conveying the impression that nothing can stop each author once he has embarked on his rehearsal of the riches that we possess in Christ.

We can profitably allow this entry to prompt us to reflect on the subject of this entire anthology and to buoy us up appropriately. ■

Galatians 1:3–4 is a beautiful finale to the medley that constitutes this entry: "Grace to you and peace from God the Father and the Lord Jesus Christ, who gave himself for our sins to deliver us from the present evil age."

Jacopo Tintoretto, *The Conversion of Saint Paul*, ca. 1544

Glory to the Lamb

SELECTIONS FROM THE BOOK OF REVELATION

John the Apostle to the Seven Churches

Grace to you and peace,
from Jesus Christ the faithful witness,
  the firstborn of the dead,
  and the ruler of kings on earth.
To him who loves us
  and has freed us from our sins by his blood
and made us a kingdom,
  priests to his God and Father,
to him be glory and dominion forever and ever. Amen.

The Lord Jesus

Fear not, I am the first and the last,
  and the living one.
I died, and behold I am alive forevermore.

The Elders

Worthy are you,
  our Lord and God,
to receive glory and honor and power.

Worthy are you to take the scroll
  and to open its seals,
for you were slain,
  and by your blood you ransomed people for God
from every tribe and language
  and people and nation,
and you have made them a kingdom
  and priests to our God,
and they shall reign on the earth.

The Angel

They have washed their robes
  and made them white in the blood of the Lamb.
The Lamb in the midst of the throne
  will be their shepherd,
and he will guide them to springs of living water,
  and God will wipe away every tear from their eyes.

Let us rejoice and exult
  and give him the glory,
for the marriage of the Lamb has come,
  and his Bride has made herself ready;
it was granted her to clothe herself
  with fine linen, bright and pure—
for the fine linen is the righteous deeds of the saints.
Blessed are those who are invited
  to the marriage supper of the Lamb.

John the Apostle

And I saw no temple in the city,
  for its temple is the Lord God the Almighty
  and the Lamb.
And the city has no need of sun or moon
  to shine on it,
for the glory of God gives it light,
  and its lamp is the Lamb.

The Lord Jesus

Behold, I am coming soon,
  bringing my recompense with me.
Blessed are those who wash their robes,
  so that they may have the right
  to enter the city by the gates. ■

THE UNIFYING THEME OF THIS poetic collage is how worthy the risen Christ is to receive glory. The poem fits the New Testament genre of the *Christ hymn*. It expresses an effusion of praise by means of an electrifying outpouring of adoration that sweeps us into its orb. Within this unifying rhapsody, we find a pleasing variety as well. Some of the stanzas are spoken by Christ himself, some by characters in the book of Revelation, and some by all believers.

If we shift our attention from the elements of form to the content, we can see two ways in which the passage sums up this anthology. Part of the time, its focus is on Jesus' sacrificial death—a death that is actually a supreme victory. At other moments, it makes us aware of Jesus'

Christ and the Virgin Enthroned with Forty Saints (detail), ca. 1340

resurrection, as he is alive and active in the pages of Revelation. As we live with the poem, we come to see that it puts an equal emphasis on death and immortality.

The passage's content is conveyed, as the content of poetry always is, through images and metaphors. The main image is that of Christ as a Lamb. This biblical *archetype* (recurrent symbol) denotes Christ's role as the atoning sacrifice whose blood secures the salvation of believers. But this divine Lamb is also the head of a great spiritual kingdom of followers. On the human side, the dominant archetype is that of white garments. These garments are symbols of redemption, and of our future glorification in heaven, but paradoxically they have been made white by the blood of the Lamb. All these images will yield deeper and deeper spiritual meanings as we contemplate them.

Even though the foreground action in the poem is affective or emotional, there is no shortage of theological reflection. One strand is the motif of blood sacrifice as the foundation of redemption, which echoes the sentiment of Hebrews 9:22 that "under the law almost everything is purified with blood, and without the shedding of blood there is no forgiveness of sins." The glorification of saints in heaven is a second theological thread woven into the tapestry of the poem, elaborated with an explosion of evocative images such as springs of living water, bright and pure garments, a festive marriage supper, and resplendent light.

An important further dimension to this poem arises from the fact that it appears in the last book of the Bible. As we read the Old Testament prophecies about the Suffering Servant and the gospel accounts of the passion of Jesus, we are weighed down by the sadness of what is happening. But in the *eschaton* (the last day) pictured in this poem, there is no room for sadness. Instead everything is a grand victory.

The passage achieves its devotional purpose as we abandon ourselves to the rapture that it expresses. ■

Underlying the rhapsody of this poem is the narrative of Christ's conquest in Revelation 19:

> Then I saw heaven opened, and behold, a white horse! The one sitting on it is called Faithful and True. . . . He is clothed in a robe dipped in blood. . . . On his robe and on his thigh he has a name written, King of kings and Lord of lords" (vv. 11, 13, 16).

RETROSPECTIVE

The entries in this anthology have been individual meditations on Jesus' atoning death on the cross and his resurrection from the grave. How might we bind these individual statements into a coherent whole? Equally, what do the death and resurrection of Jesus look like when they are codified as a statement of belief?

The Apostles' Creed provides a ready answer to both questions. ■

Twenty-Two Houses and a Church, mid 19th century

I Believe

The Apostles' Creed

I believe in God the Father almighty,
maker of heaven and earth;

And in Jesus Christ his only Son our Lord, who was
conceived by the Holy Ghost,
born of the Virgin Mary,
suffered under Pontius Pilate,
was crucified, dead and buried;
he descended into hell;
the third day he rose again from the dead;
he ascended into heaven,
and sits on the right hand of God the Father almighty;
from thence he shall come to judge the living and the dead.

I believe in
the Holy Spirit;
the holy catholic church;
the communion of saints;
the forgiveness of sins;
the resurrection of the body,
and the life everlasting. ■

Two preliminary questions deserve to be raised and answered. First, can the Apostles' Creed be read devotionally? It can. When we recite it in a church service, we are kept moving at an exhilarating march. But the creed lends itself to devotional meditation as well. Each item within it deserves to be dwelled upon. Second, is the Apostles' Creed prose or poetry? Its abundance of short parallel clauses and phrases creates the effect of a poetic composition. Even when the Apostles' Creed is not printed as it is here, nonetheless it is structured on the poetic principle of short lines that feature the additional artistic principles of repetition and parallelism.

The Apostles' Creed is an apt retrospective for this anthology in several ways. Because it is comprehensive, it enables us to see the redemptive life of Christ in the context of the broader story of salvation history. The dominance of Christ in the creed illustrates the christological nature of Christian belief, without undermining its Trinitarian nature as well. The individual items in the section of the creed that is devoted to Jesus are arranged according to the chronology of his redemptive life. In other words, they tell a story as well as summarize what we believe. That story follows a U-shaped contour that descends into potential tragedy and then rises to a triumphant conclusion. A further way in which the creed sums up this anthology is that after it declares what Jesus did (redemption accomplished), it asserts in its final section the effects of his actions in the lives of believers (redemption applied)—the same template that has organized the entire anthology.

Apostles in Prayer, ca. 1400–10

The structure of the middle section of the creed is an amazing achievement. We find five statements about Jesus that complete the verb *was* (*conceived, born, crucified, dead, buried*). That series is followed by four parallel clauses that name what Jesus did following his resurrection, and these four actions have the additional nuance of covering the past (*rose, ascended*), present (*sits on the right hand of God*), and future (*shall come to judge*). When we recite the creed, we experience an emotional descent that takes us down, down, down until we reach the dolorous line *he descended into hell*. The line stating that *the third day he rose again from the dead* provides a sudden uplift, after which our emotions soar up, up, up.

As we meditate on the individual statements of belief and the overall shape of the Apostles' Creed, we can relive Holy Week in capsule form. ■

The Bible itself contains an apostles' creed in miniature:

> [Christ] was manifested in the flesh,
> vindicated by the Spirit,
> seen by angels,
> proclaimed among the nations,
> believed on in the world,
> taken up in glory. (1 Tim. 3:16)

Raphael, *Eight Apostles*, ca. 1514

Notes

MOST OF THE EXTERNAL FACTS that are attached to the poems in this anthology belong to a common storehouse. This information appears in numerous sources, both print and electronic, making it misleading to attach it to a specific source. Whenever information for a given entry is tied to a specific source, or when I judged that a reader might want further details, I have provided a note.

The selections from the Book of Common Prayer were gleaned from different parts and editions of the book and lightly edited by Leland Ryken.

The excerpt from Milton's *Paradise Lost* is taken from book 3, lines 138–43, 150–58, 160–64, 167–80, 203, 209–19, 222–28, 236–43, 245, 247–52. The quotation from Athanasius appears in *On the Incarnation of the Word of God,* trans. T. Herbert Bindley (London: The Religious Tract Society, 1905). The quotation from Thomas Chalmers appears in William Hannah, *Memoirs of Thomas Chalmers* (Edinburgh, 1854), 2:72.

The detailed outline that appears in the explication of Philippians 2:5–11 replicates chapter titles in Ralph P. Martin, *A Hymn of Christ: Philippians 2:5–11 in Recent Interpretation and in the Setting of Early Christian Worship* (Downers Grove, IL: InterVarsity Press, 1997).

The Old Testament passages in the Psalm for Palm Sunday are as follows: Zech. 9:9; Ps. 118:15–16, 19–20, 26; Ps. 92:12; Ps. 2:6; Ps. 8:2; Is. 9:7; 2 Sam. 7:12, 16 (footnote); Isa. 12:2–3, 5–6.

"All Glory, Laud, and Honor" was composed in Latin in 820 by the Catholic bishop Theodulf. It was written in thirty-nine couplets, much longer than the English version by John Mason Neale, the great Victorian

A Passional (detail),
end of 15th century or early 16th century

translator of hymns of the ancient church. When Neale's translation was first published in *Hymns Ancient and Modern* in 1851, it was packaged as six four-line stanzas; the more ponderous eight-line stanzas with which we are familiar are required by the tune that is associated with it in nearly all modern hymnbooks.

"'Tis Midnight, and on Olive's Brow" was first published in 1822, under the title "Gethsemane." The quotations from Harriet Beecher Stowe in the explication come from her book *Footsteps of the Master* (New York, 1877).

The story of Fanny Crosby's conversion while singing the concluding words of "Alas! and Did My Savior Bleed" is described in her memoir, *Memories of Eighty Years* (Boston: James H. Earle & Company, 1906), 96.

Jacob Revius's poem "He Bore Our Griefs" is reproduced from *Jacobus Revius: Dutch Metaphysical Poet,* ed. and trans. Henrietta Ten Harmsel (Detroit: Wayne State University Press, 1968), 115.

Among sources that link the composition of "And Can It Be?" to Wesley's reading of Luther's commentary on Galatians is John R. Tyson, *Assist Me to Proclaim: The Life and Hymns of Charles Wesley* (Grand Rapids: Eerdmans, 2007), 49. William Wordsworth's theory that lyric poetry exists to rectify people's feelings and give them new compositions of feeling is found in his letter "Of the Principles of Poetry and His Own Poems," in *The Prose Works of William Wordsworth,* vol. 2, *Aesthetical and Literary,* ed. Alexander B. Grosart (London, 1876), 211.

The original title of "There Is a Fountain Filled with Blood," as well as its link to Zechariah 13:1 when it was first printed, is found in John Newton, *Olney Hymns, in Three Books* (London, 1779), 98.

Joseph Addison's own linking of his poem "When Rising from the Bed of Death" with his illness is from the October 18, 1712, issue of his magazine *The Spectator,* as reprinted in Alexander Chalmers, ed. *The Spectator: A New Edition, Carefully Revised* (New York, 1853), 5:518.

"The Old Rugged Cross" is one of the most storied hymns in existence, and the information that appears in the commentary of this anthology is a conflation of material that can be found in many places. For readers who wish

Master of the Figdor Deposition,
The Crucifixion, ca. 1505

to pursue the subject, one good representative webpage is Chris Fenner, "The Old Rugged Cross," Hymnology Archive, last updated August 2, 2002, https://www.hymnologyarchive.com/the-old-rugged-cross.

"The Day of Resurrection!" and "Come, Ye Faithful, Raise the Strain" were originally composed by a monk who lived near Jerusalem in the late seventh and early eighth centuries. This monk, John of Damascus, was a towering "Greek Father" and an important theological influence on the Eastern church.

The entry on our resurrection on the last day is taken from 1 Corinthians 15:20–26, 39–49, 51–53.

The selections from the Epistles on the believer's riches in Christ are the following: Ephesians 1:3, 7; Colossians 1:12–14; Titus 3:4–7; Hebrews 13:20–21; 1 Peter 1:3–5; 2 Peter 1:3–4, 11.

The selections from the book of Revelation that give glory to the Lamb are as follows: 1:4–6, 17–18; 4:11; 5:9–10; 7:14, 17; 19:7–9; 21:22–23; 22:12, 14.

Penitent Mary Magdalene, 1700–1800

Image Credits

Unless noted by a Creative Commons license, the following artworks are in public domain. All artworks have been reproduced in good faith, recognizing copyrights where required. Many images have been cropped to fit the format of this book..

Special thanks are due to the following museums for providing artwork and helpful information: Alte Pinakothek (Munich), Art Institute of Chicago, Barnes Foundation (Philadelphia), Bonnefantenmuseum (Maastricht), Detroit Institute of Arts, Kröller-Müller Museum (Otterlo), Metropolitan Museum of Art (New York), National Gallery of Art (Washington, DC), National Library of Wales (Aberystwyth), National Museum (Kraków), Philadelphia Museum of Art, Rijksmuseum (Amsterdam), State Russian Museum (Saint Petersburg), and Walters Art Museum (Baltimore).

5 Eric Gill, *The Resurrection*, 1917, wood engraving on cream wove paper, Art Institute of Chicago, www.artic.edu.

6 Gerbrand van den Eeckhout, *The Last Supper*, 1664, oil on canvas, Rijksmuseum, Amsterdam, www.rijksmuseum.nl.

8–9 Attributed to Pieter Brueghel the Younger, *The Crucifixion*, ca. 1617, oil on panel, Philadelphia Museum of Art, www.philamuseum.org.

10 Master of the Death of Saint Nicholas of Münster, *Calvary*, ca. 1470/80, oil on panel, National Gallery of Art, www.nga.gov.

13 Benjamin West, *Angel of the Resurrection*, 1801, pen-and-tusche lithograph, National Gallery of Art, Washington, DC, www.nga.gov.

16 Detail from Fernando Gallego and workshop, *The Agony in the Garden*, 1480–88, oil on panel, University of Arizona Museum of Art, Tucson. Daderot / Wikimedia Commons / CC0 1.0. https://creativecommons.org/licenses/by/1.0/.

21 Georges de La Tour, *The Repentant Magdalen*, ca. 1635/40, oil on canvas, National Gallery of Art, Washington, DC, www.nga.gov.

22 Maximilian Wolf, *The Milky Way*, ca. 1900, gelatin silver print, National Gallery of Art, Washington, DC, www.nga.gov.

27 Benjamin West, *The Expulsion of Adam and Eve from Paradise*, 1791, oil on canvas, National Gallery of Art, Washington, DC, www.nga.gov.

31 Copy after Paulus Potter, *Bellowing Bull*, 17th century, oil on canvas, Philadelphia Museum of Art, www.philamuseum.org.

33 Robert Hills (1769–1844), *Five Sheep*, no date, graphite on wove paper, National Gallery of Art, Washington, DC, www.nga.gov.

Gerbrand van den Eeckhout, *The Last Supper*, 1664

35 Rene Romero Schuler, *Shadow*, 2012, acrylic on canvas, Wikimedia Commons / CC-BY-SA-3.0. https://creativecommons.org/licenses/by-sa/3.0/. Cropped and colors adjusted.

36 Lid of box, 1830–70, parian porcelain, Metropolitan Museum of Art, New York, www.metmuseum.org.

38 *Saints and Worshippers in Adoration*, 1510/15, glass, vitreous paint, silver stain, and lead, Art Institute of Chicago, www.artic.edu.

40 Rodrigo de Osona the Elder, *The Agony in the Garden*, ca. 1465, oil and gold on panel, Philadelphia Museum of Art, www.philamuseum.org.

44–45 Pieter Coecke van Aelst, *Entry into Jerusalem*, ca. 1530–35, oil on oak panel, Bonnefantenmuseum, Maastricht, www.bonnefanten.nl.

47–48 Jan Luyken, *Intocht in Jerusalem* [Entry into Jerusalem], 1712, etching on paper, Rijksmuseum, Amsterdam, www.rijksmuseum.nl.

50 Detail from School of Florence, *The Agony in the Garden*, 1320, tempera on wood panel, Detroit Institute of Arts, www.dia.org.

52 Luis Meléndez, *Still Life with Figs and Bread*, ca. 1770, oil on canvas, National Gallery of Art, Washington, DC, www.nga.gov.

54 Ugolino da Siena, *The Last Supper*, ca. 1325–30, tempera and gold on wood, Metropolitan Museum of Art, New York, www.metmuseum.org.

57–58 Thomas Moran, *Mountain of the Holy Cross*, 1890, watercolor and gouache over graphite on paper, National Gallery of Art, Washington, DC, www.nga.gov.

60 Simon Moulijn, *Gekruisigde op rots* [Crucifixion on Rock], 1901, print on paper, Rijksmuseum, Amsterdam, www.rijksmuseum.nl.

62 Claude Déruet, *Road to Calvary*, 1615/20, oil on copper, National Gallery of Art, Washington, DC, www.nga.gov.

65 Detail from *Tłocznia Mistyczna z Lelowa* [Mystical Winepress from Lelów], 1647, oil on canvas, National Museum, Kraków, www.zbiory.mnk.pl.

66 Fritz Boehmer, *Wine Jug*, ca. 1939, watercolor, graphite, colored pencil, gouache, pen and ink, National Gallery of Art, Washington, DC, www.nga.gov.

68 Detail from Rembrandt, *Die Kreuzaufrichtung* [The Raising of the Cross], ca. 1633, oil on canvas, Alte Pinakothek, Munich, https://www.sammlung.pinakothek.de.

71 Jusepe de Ribera, *Penitent Saint Peter*, 1628/32, oil on canvas, Art Institute of Chicago, www.artic.edu.

72 Étienne Bobillet and Paul Mosselman, *Mourner*, ca. 1453, alabaster with traces of gilding, Metropolitan Museum of Art, New York, www.metmuseum.org.

74 Govert Flinck, *Isaac Blessing Jacob*, ca. 1638, oil on canvas, Rijksmuseum, Amsterdam, www.rijksmuseum.nl.

77 Victor-François-Eloi Biennourry, *The Mocking of Christ*, 1852, black chalk with white heightening on two joined pieces of blue paper, National Gallery of Art, Washington, DC, www.nga.gov.

81 Jacopo Bassano, *The Mocking of Christ*, 1568, colored chalks on blue laid paper, National Gallery of Art, Washington, DC, www.nga.gov.

83 Probably Constantijn van Renesse, *The Descent from the Cross*, 1650/52, oil on canvas, National Gallery of Art, Washington, DC, www.nga.gov.

85 Jacopo di Cione, *Saint Peter Released from Prison*, 1370–71, tempera and tooled gold on panel, Philadelphia Museum of Art, www.philamuseum.org.

87 Alphonse Legros (1837–1911), *Choir of a Spanish Church*, no date, charcoal, National Gallery of Art, Washington, DC, www.nga.gov.

88 Gospel leaf depicting the Fountain of Life, first half 14th century, tempera on parchment, Metropolitan Museum of Art, New York, www.metmuseum.org.

89 Mätre Krestos, Crucifixion from the Ethiopian Gospels, early 14th century, ink and paint on heavy, yellow parchment, Walters Art Museum, Baltimore, art.thewalters.org.

91 Details from Viktor Mikhaylovich Vasnetsov, *The Last Judgment*, 1885–96, oil on canvas,

93 Giovanni Baronzio, *The Baptism of Christ*, ca. 1335, tempera on panel, National Gallery of Art, Washington, DC, www.nga.gov.

97 Juan de Flandes, *Crucifixion*, ca. 1490, oil on panel, Barnes Foundation, Philadelphia, collection.barnesfoundation.org.

98–99 Alphonse Legros (1837–1911), *At the Foot of the Cross*, no date, pen and brown ink with brown wash over graphite on laid paper, National Gallery of Art, Washington, DC, www.nga.gov.

101 Mourners and Soldiers from a Crucifixion, late 15th century, alabaster with traces of paint, Metropolitan Museum of Art, New York, www.metmuseum.org.

103 Totoya Hokkei, *A Mountainous Landscape with a Stream*, 1827, color woodblock print, Art Institute of Chicago, www.artic.edu.

104 Frederic Edwin Church, *El Rio de Luz* [The River of Light], 1877, oil on canvas, National Gallery of Art, Washington, DC, www.nga.gov.

107 *Crucifixion*, early 1400s, Ohrid Icon Gallery, St. Mary Bolnichka Church, commons.wikimedia.org.

111 Edvard Munch, *The Sun*, 1911, oil on canvas, University of Oslo, www.uio.no, commons.wikimedia.org.

112 Boëtius Adamsz Bolswert, *Engel verschijnt voor de drie Maria's bij het lege graf* [An Angel Appears before the Three Marys at the Tomb], 1590–1622, engraving on paper, Rijksmuseum, Amsterdam, www.rijksmuseum.nl.

115 Plaque with the Holy Women at the Sepulchre, ca. 1140–60, walrus ivory, Metropolitan Museum of Art, New York, www.metmuseum.org.

117 Copy after David Teniers II, *Wedding Feast*, late 17th century, oil on panel, Philadelphia Museum of Art, www.philamuseum.org.

118 Jean-Baptiste Patas, after drawing by Jean-Baptiste Joseph Wicar, after painting by Pietro da Cortona, *Drie Maria's bij het lege graf* [Three Marys at the Empty Tomb], 1789–1807, engraving on paper, Rijksmuseum, Amsterdam, www.rijksmuseum.nl.

119–20 Guglielmus Paludanus, *The Resurrection*, 1565–1665, alabaster with traces of red bole, gilding and silvering, Rijksmuseum, Amsterdam, www.rijksmuseum.nl.

123 Vincent van Gogh, *Korenveld met maaier en zon* [Wheat Field with Reaper and Sun], 1889, oil on canvas, Kröller-Müller Museum, Otterlo, www.krollermuller.nl.

Claus Sluter, *Calvary*, ca. 1390–1410

125 A. A. Ivanov, *Явление Христа Марии Магдалине после Воскресения* [Christ's Appearance to Mary Magdalene after the Resurrection], 1835, oil on canvas, State Russian Museum, Saint Petersburg,www.rusmuseumvrm.ru.

126 Erasmus Quellinus II, *Saint Thomas Touching Christ's Wounds,* 1644, oil on panel, Philadelphia Museum of Art, www.philamuseum.org.

128–29 He Qi, *Resurrection,* no date. Used with permission. www.heqiart.com.

131 Lidia Kozenitzky, *KriatYamSoof,* 2009, https://commons.wikimedia.org/wiki/User:Effib.

132 Jan Luyken (1660–1712), *Het Pascha* [The Passover], no date, ink on paper, Rijksmuseum, Amsterdam, www.rijksmuseum.nl.

135 Jan Luyken, *De hemelpoort* [Heaven's Gate], 1708–10, ink on paper, Rijksmuseum, Amsterdam, www.rijksmuseum.nl.

136 Charles Mottram after John Martin, *The Plains of Heaven,* 1857, hand-colored mezzotint with etching and engraving, printed in color on wove paper, National Gallery of Art, Washington, DC, www.nga.gov.

138–39 Paul Cézanne, *Nature morte au crâne* [Still Life with Skull], 1890–93, oil on canvas, Barnes Foundation, Philadelphia, collection.barnesfoundation.org.

143 Jan Lievens, *The Resurrection of Lazarus,* 1620–74, etching, Metropolitan Museum of Art, New York, www.metmuseum.org.

146–47 Jacopo Tintoretto, *The Conversion of Saint Paul,* ca. 1544, oil on canvas, National Gallery of Art, Washington, DC, www.nga.gov.

150 Detail from *Christ and the Virgin Enthroned with Forty Saints,* ca. 1340, miniature on vellum, National Gallery of Art, Washington, DC, www.nga.gov.

152 *Twenty-Two Houses and a Church,* mid 19th century, water-based medium on canvas, National Gallery of Art, Washington, DC, www.nga.gov.

155 *Apostles in Prayer,* ca. 1400–10, oak, Metropolitan Museum of Art, New York, www.metmuseum.org.

156 Raphael, *Eight Apostles*, ca. 1514, red chalk over stylus underdrawing and traces of leadpoint on laid paper, National Gallery of Art, Washington, DC, www.nga.gov.

157 Detail from *A Passional*, end of 15th century or early 16th century, illuminated manuscript, f.17.v, National Library of Wales, Aberystwyth, https://viewer.library.wales/4399684#.

158 Master of the Figdor Deposition, *The Crucifixion*, ca. 1505, oil on panel, Rijksmuseum, Amsterdam, www.rijksmuseum.nl.

160 *Boetvaardige Maria Magdalena* [Penitent Mary Magdalene], 1700–1800, oil on paper, Rijksmuseum, Amsterdam, www.rijksmuseum.nl.

162 Gerbrand van den Eeckhout, *The Last Supper*, 1664, oil on canvas, Rijksmuseum, Amsterdam, www.rijksmuseum.nl.

165 Claus Sluter, *Calvary*, ca. 1390–1410, boxwood, Rijksmuseum, Amsterdam, www.rijksmuseum.nl.

166–67 Two groups of horsemen from a crucifixion scene, ca. 1440, oak with polychromy, gilding, leather, glass and metal, Rijksmuseum, Amsterdam, www.rijksmuseum.nl.

168 Jean Bourdichon, *The Pentecost*, ca. 1480, tempera, granular gold paint, inscribed brown ink, pen and ink, and gilding on parchment, Barnes Foundation, Philadelphia, collection.barnesfoundation.org.

Two groups of horsemen from a crucifixion scene, ca. 1440

Scripture Index

Jean Bourdichon, *The Pentecost*, ca. 1480